THE BEST IN TENT CAMPING

THE CAROLINAS

FIRST EDITION

Other Books by Johnny Molloy

Beach and Coastal Camping in Florida
The Best in Tent Camping: Colorado
The Best in Tent Camping: Florida
The Best in Camping: Georgia
The Best in Tent Camping: The Southern Appalachian and Smoky Mountains
The Best in Tent Camping: Tennessee and Kentucky
The Best in Tent Camping: West Virginia
The Best in Tent Camping: Wisconsin
Day and Overnight Hikes in the Great Smoky Mountains National Park
Day and Overnight Hikes in the Shenandoah National Park
Day and Overnight Hikes in West Virginia's Monongahela National Forest
From the Swamp to the Keys: A Paddle through Florida History
The Hiking Trails of Florida's National Forests, Parks, and Preserves
Land Between the Lakes Outdoor Recreation Handbook
Long Trails of the Southeast
Mount Rogers Outdoor Recreation Handbook
A Paddler's Guide to Everglades National Park
60 Hikes within 60 Miles: Austin and San Antonio (co-authored with Tom Taylor)
60 Hikes within 60 Miles: Nashville
Trial by Trail: Backpacking in the Smoky Mountains

Visit the author's website:
www.johnnymolloy.com

THE BEST IN TENT CAMPING

A GUIDE FOR CAR CAMPERS WHO HATE RVs, CONCRETE SLABS, AND LOUD PORTABLE STEREOS

THE CAROLINAS

FIRST EDITION

JOHNNY MOLLOY

MENASHA RIDGE PRESS
BIRMINGHAM, ALABAMA

This book is for residents of North Carolina and South Carolina,
who enjoy some great places to live, work, and tent camp.

Copyright © 2003 by Johnny Molloy

All rights reserved

Printed in the United States of America

Published by Menasha Ridge Press

Distributed by the Globe Pequot Press

First edition, first printing

Library of Congress Cataloging in Publication

Molloy, Johnny, 1961—

    The best in tent camping, the Carolinas: a guide for campers who hate RVs, concrete slabs, and loud portable stereos / Johnny Molloy.—1st ed.

p.cm.

Includes index

    ISBN 0-89732-547-8

    1. Camping—North Carolina—Guidebooks. 2. Campsites, facilities, etc.—North Carolina—Guidebooks. 3. North Carolina—Guidebooks. 4. Camping—South Carolina—Guidebooks. 5. Campsites, facilities, etc.—South Carolina—Guidebooks. 6. South Carolina—Guidebooks. I. Title.

GV191.42.N3M65 2003

796.54′09756—dc21

2003051373
CIP

Cover and text design by Ian Szymkowiak, Palace Press International, Inc.

Cover photo by Ernest H. Robl

Menasha Ridge Press

P.O. Box 43673

Birmingham, Alabama 35243

www.menasharidge.com

TABLE OF CONTENTS

KEY TO CAMPGROUND LOCATOR MAPS

NORTH CAROLINA MOUNTAINS

1 BALSAM MOUNTAIN
2 BIG CREEK
3 CABLE COVE
4 CATALOOCHEE
5 DOUGHTON
6 HANGING DOG
7 HORSE COVE
8 LAKE JAMES STATE PARK
9 LINVILLE FALLS
10 MOUNT MITCHELL STATE PARK
11 NELSON'S NANTAHALA HIDEAWAY
12 NEW RIVER STATE PARK
13 NORTH MILLS RIVER
14 PRICE PARK
15 ROCKY BLUFF
16 STANDING INDIAN
17 STONE MOUNTAIN STATE PARK
18 SOUTH MOUNTAINS STATE PARK
19 SUNBURST
20 TSALI

NORTH CAROLINA PIEDMONT

21 BADIN LAKE
22 HANGING ROCK
23 LAKE NORMAN STATE PARK
24 MORROW MOUNTAIN STATE PARK
25 PILOT MOUNTAIN STATE PARK
26 WEST MORRIS MOUNTAIN

NORTH CAROLINA COAST AND COASTAL PLAIN

27 CAROLINA BEACH STATE PARK
28 CLIFFS OF THE NEUSE STATE PARK
29 FRISCO

30 GOOSE CREEK STATE PARK
31 JONES LAKE STATE PARK
32 LUMBER RIVER STATE PARK
33 MERCHANTS MILLPOND STATE PARK
34 NEUSE RIVER
35 OCRACOKE

SOUTH CAROLINA UPCOUNTRY

36 BURRELLS FORD
37 CHERRY HILL
38 DEVILS FORK STATE PARK
39 JONES GAP STATE PARK
40 KEOWEE–TOXAWAY STATE PARK
41 OCONEE STATE PARK
42 SADLERS CREEK STATE RECREATION AREA
43 TABLE ROCK STATE PARK

SOUTH CAROLINA MIDLANDS

44 BRICK HOUSE
45 CALHOUN FALLS STATE RECREATION AREA
46 KINGS MOUNTAIN STATE PARK
47 LEROY'S FERRY
48 LICK FORK LAKE
49 PARSONS MOUNTAIN
50 SAND HILLS STATE FOREST
51 WOODS FERRY

SOUTH CAROLINA LOWCOUNTRY

52 HONEY HILL
53 HUNTING ISLAND STATE PARK
54 HUNTINGTON BEACH STATE PARK
55 LITTLE PEE DEE STATE PARK

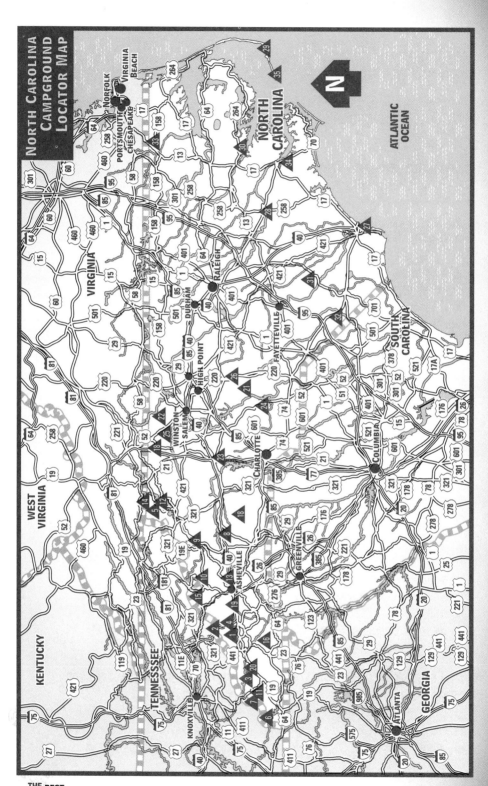

NORTH CAROLINA CAMPGROUND LOCATOR MAP

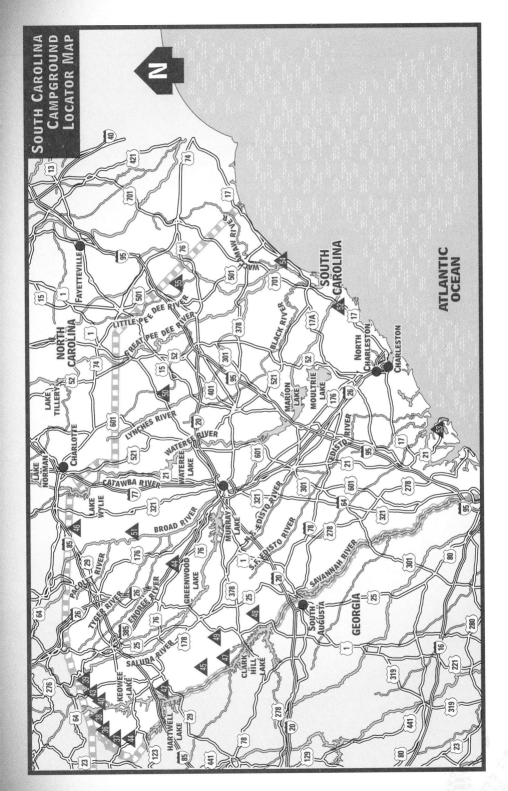

ACKNOWLEDGMENTS

I WOULD LIKE TO THANK all of the land managers of North and South Carolina's state parks and forests and the folks at the national forests for helping me in the research and writing of this book.

Thanks to Lisa Daniel for camping with me and keeping me company at campgrounds and at home. Thanks to Aaron Marable for hiking with me on the Buncombe Trail, to Cisco Meyer for camping with me at Oconee State Park, and to Steve Grayson and John Bland for going to the Tennessee-South Carolina football game in Columbia. Thanks to Linda Grebe at Eureka! for providing me with great tents both big and small. Thanks to Silva for their compasses and Camp Trails for their packs. Thanks to travelin' Jean Cobb and motorcyclin' Brooke Wilson at Freebairn & Co. for their help.

The biggest thanks of all goes to the people of North Carolina and South Carolina. They have beautiful and historic states in which to tent camp.

PREFACE

B**EING A SOUTHERNER,** I jumped at the opportunity to write *The Best in Tent Camping: The Carolinas*. Having traveled extensively through and written about the mountainous regions of North Carolina and South Carolina, I looked at writing this book as an excuse to thoroughly and systematically explore the remainder of the two states, tent camping, of course. With a Eureka! tent and laptop computer in my Jeep, I took off, exploring by day and tent camping at night, breaking out the computer to type up on-site reports about each destination. My high expectations were exceeded. I knew the islands and beaches were beautiful from past visits, but have you been to the Outer Banks in fall, with a cool breeze and warm golden light spilling onto its sands? Have you explored the rich, forested interior of Hunting Island, then looked out from atop its lighthouse? To me, what lay between the Atlantic beaches and the Appalachian range was most surprising.

In North Carolina, Merchants Millpond State Park features a swamp not unlike the famed Okefenokee Swamp of Georgia. The Lumber River also has dark water and is a federally designated wild and scenic river. The Piedmont has the Uwharrie National Forest, where hiking trails wind beneath verdant forested hills broken by clear streams. Where the Piedmont meets the hills stands Pilot Mountain. Have you ever seen Pilot Mountain, with its cylindrical, flat-topped cone rising 1,400 feet above the surrounding landscape?

In South Carolina, the pleasant surprises started in the Francis Marion National Forest, just a few miles inland from the Atlantic Ocean. This locale offers nature study amid wooded wetlands and canoe routes through some of the least-trammeled terrain in the Palmetto State. Sand Hills State Forest harbors an ecosystem unique to the Carolinas. The varied tracts of the Sumter National Forest in the Midlands offer great recreational opportunities. The Buncombe Trail, now a South Carolina favorite of mine, circles sleepy Brick House Campground. Lick Fork Lake is an ideal mix of campground and land- and water-based recreation located in an attractive setting. Leroy's Ferry Campground, operated by the Army Corps of Engineers, was a quiet respite on big Thurmond Lake.

Even the mountains offered some new surprises, like the New River in the northwest corner of North Carolina. This ancient watercourse winds its way through steep hills, offering excellent canoeing and fishing for smallmouth bass. For forays onto the river, use the Wagoner Unit of New River State Park as a base camp. The walk-in tent camping sites at South Carolina's Oconee State Park make for shaded hideaways between walking treks on the Foothills Trail and the nearby paths it intersects.

Time passed, though, and the explorations sadly ended. With the aid of the helpful folks at Menasha Ridge Press, this book has now come to be. But I made many wonderful memories along the way, and expect to make many more in the Carolinas. I hope this book will help you make some memories of your own.

— *Johnny Molloy*

CAMPGROUND MAPS
LEGEND

WHITE WOLF

◬

Campground name
and location

▲24 ▲ 🚐

Individual Tent and RV
campsites within
campground area

Table Rock

◬

Other nearby
campgrounds

NATIONAL   STATE
FOREST   PARK

Public lands

≡〔64〕≡

Interstate
highways

=〔19〕〔219〕=

U.S.
highways

════════

Other roads

▬▬▬▬▬

Unpaved or
gravel roads

▪▪▪▪▪▪▪▪▪▪▪

Boardwalk

▬▬▬▬▬

Political
boundary

+++++++++

Railroads

─ ─ ─ ─ ─

Hiking, biking,
or horse trail

Swift Creek

River or stream

Asheville

●

City
or town

N

Indicates North

Ward Lake

Ocean, lake,
or bay

⚊ Bridge or tunnel

(ⁱ⁾ Amphitheater

🦟 Falls or rapids

⬛ Food

👫 Restroom

🚰 Water Access

▱ Gate

🗑 Trash disposal

🛝 Playground

🚗 Parking

◱ Marina or boat ramp

🔥 Fire ring

☎ Telephone

◯ Laundry

✝ Cemetery

🏊 Swimming

🜨 Picnic area

🏔 Sheltered
Picnic area

◗ Spring/Well

⬠ Dishwater disposal

▲ Summit
or lookout

⬛ Bath House

▦ Trailer Dumpsite

🚫 No Swimming

THE BEST IN TENT CAMPING

A GUIDE FOR CAR CAMPERS WHO HATE RVs, CONCRETE SLABS, AND LOUD PORTABLE STEREOS

THE CAROLINAS

INTRODUCTION

NORTH AND SOUTH CAROLINA offer varied and scenic ecosystems overlain with a rich human history. Both states stretch from the alluring Blue Ridge Mountains in the west—the highest, and some would argue, the most scenic range of the Appalachians—to the saltwater washed sands of the Atlantic coast in the east. These Southern Appalachians, unmatched in biodiversity in temperate climes, offer shady forests through which clear streams dance over gray boulders, feeding rivers that race toward the Piedmont. Here, where the hills soften, the beauty is more subtle, yet clearly alive to the discerning camper. Enhancing this natural charm, many rivers have been impounded to offer the tent camper endless water recreation opportunities. The central lands give way to the coastal plain where dark rivers quietly flow among buttressed cypress trees. Moving east, the water of the mountains meets the water of the sea, forming rich estuarine habitats, further complementing the ecosystem. Finally, the land ends at the Atlantic Ocean's edge, bordered by slender sand island chains and shell dotted beaches.

It is in the Carolinas where much of our country's formative history took place. For starters, did you know more Revolutionary battles between the Americans and the British took place in South Carolina than in any other state—or that the first English-speaking colonies in North America were located in North Carolina? In fact, under a charter from Queen Elizabeth, Sir Walter Raleigh initiated two North Carolina colonies in the 1580s. It is this melding of human and natural history that makes exploring the Carolinas so appealing.

Today tent campers can enjoy each of these distinct regions of the Carolinas. At the lofty altitude of 6,320 feet in Mount Mitchell State Park, you can pitch your tent at the highest campground in the East. Or camp along a federally designated Wild and Scenic river, such as the Chattooga or the New. The central Carolinas has quiet Woods Ferry, where Civil War soldiers once crossed the Broad River and where you can rejoin nature at West Morris Mountain. Here also are the big waters of Lake Norman State Park, where you can camp on a peninsula nearly encircled by the lake. The coastal plain also has scenic rivers ready to be explored, such as the Lumber and Little Pee Dee. A tent camper has to take a ferry to reach Ocracoke Campground. And there is Frisco Campground, about as far east as you can tent camp in the Carolinas, where tall dunes of sand rise high. All this spells paradise for the tent camper. No matter where you go, the scenery will never fail to please the eye.

Before embarking on a trip, take time to prepare. Many of the best tent campgrounds are a fair distance from the civilized world and you'll want to enjoy yourself rather than make supply or gear runs. Call ahead and ask for a park map, brochure, or other information to help you plan your trip. Visit campground websites for more information. Make reservations wherever applicable, especially at popular state parks, and don't forget to inquire about the latest reservation fees and entrance fees at state parks and forests.

Ask questions. Ask more questions. Although this guidebook is an indispensable tool for the Carolina-bound tent camper, the more questions you ask, the fewer surprises you will get. There are other times, however, when you'll grab your gear and this book, hop in the car, and just wing it. This can be an adventure in its own right.

THE RATING SYSTEM

Included in this book is a rating system for the Carolina's best tent campgrounds. Certain campground attributes—beauty, site privacy, site spaciousness, quiet, security, and cleanliness/upkeep—are ranked using a star system. Five stars are ideal, one is acceptable. This system will help you find the campground that has the attributes you desire.

BEAUTY

In the best campgrounds, the fluid shapes and elements of nature—flora, water, land, and sky—have melded to create locales that seem to have been made for tent camping. The best sites are so attractive you may be tempted not to leave your outdoor home. A little campsite enhancement is necessary to make the scenic area camper-friendly, but too many reminders of civilization eliminated many a campground from inclusion in this book.

SITE PRIVACY

A little understory foliage goes a long way in making you feel comfortable once you've picked your site for the night. Fortunately there is a trend to plant natural borders between campsites if the borders don't already exist. With some trees or brush to define the sites, everyone has their personal space. Then you can go about the pleasures of tent camping without keeping up with the Joneses at the site next door—or them with you.

SITE SPACIOUSNESS

This attribute can be very important depending on how much of a gearhead you are and the size of your group. Campers with family-style tents and screen shelters need a large, flat spot. This gives them room to pitch their tent and allows them to get to the ice chest to prepare foods, while not getting burned near the fire ring. Gearheads need adequate space to show off their portable glow-in-the dark lounge chairs and other pricey gewgaws to neighbors strolling by. I just want enough room to keep my bedroom, den, and kitchen separate.

QUIET

The music of the lakes, rivers, and all the land between—the singing birds, rushing streams, waves lapping against the shoreline, wind whooshing through the trees—includes the kinds of noises tent campers associate with being in the Carolinas. In concert, the sounds of nature camouflage the sounds you don't want to hear—autos coming and going, loud neighbors, and so on.

SECURITY

Campground security is relative. A remote campground in an undeveloped area is usually safe, but don't tempt potential thieves by leaving your valuables out for all to see. Use common sense, and go with your instinct. Campground hosts are wonderful to have around, and state parks with locked gates are ideal for security. Get to know your neighbors and develop a buddy system to watch each other's belongings when possible.

CLEANLINESS/UPKEEP

I'm a stickler for this one. Nothing will sabotage a scenic campground like trash. Most of the campgrounds in this guidebook are clean. More rustic campgrounds—my favorites—usually receive less maintenance. Busy weekends and holidays will show their effects; however, don't let a little litter spoil your good time. Help clean up, and think of it as doing your part for the Carolina's natural environment.

HELPFUL HINTS

To make the most of your tent camping trip, call ahead whenever possible. If going to a state or national park, call for an informative brochure before setting out. This way you can familiarize yourself with the area. Once there, ask questions. Most stewards of the land are proud of their *terra firma* and are honored you came for a visit. They're happy to help you have the best time possible.

If traveling in the national forests of the Carolinas, call ahead and order a forest map. Not only will a map make it that much easier to reach your destination, but nearby hikes, scenic drives, waterfalls, and landmarks will be easier to find. There are forest visitor centers in addition to ranger stations. Call or visit and ask questions. When ordering a map, ask for any additional literature about the area in which you are interested.

In writing this book I had the pleasure of meeting many friendly helpful people: local residents proud of the unique lands around them, state park and national forest employees who endured my endless questions. Even better were my fellow tent campers, who were eager to share their knowledge about their favorite spots. They already know what beauty lies on the horizon. As North Carolina and South Carolina become more populated, these lands become that much more precious. Enjoy them, protect them, and use them wisely.

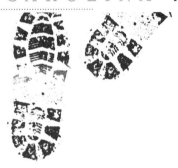

NORTH CAROLINA **MOUNTAINS**

BALSAM MOUNTAIN CAMPGROUND

THE RARE SPRUCE-FIR FORESTS that cloak the highest elevations of the Smokies are among the primary reasons the Smoky Mountains were designated a national park. Covering 13,000 of the park's 500,000 acres, this is the southern limit of this relic of the ice age. Over 10,000 years ago, when glaciers covered much of the United States, a forest much more reminiscent of those in Canada today migrated south. When the glaciers retreated, this forest survived on the highest points of the Smokies, creating an "island" forest of red spruce and Fraser fir trees.

So what does this have to do with tent camping? Well, it just so happens that Balsam Mountain Campground is located in a swath of this rare forest. So, not only does Balsam Mountain offer the highest tent camping within the confines of the Great Smoky Mountains National Park, it also offers campers a chance to experience this remarkable forest first hand.

Balsam Mountain Campground was set up not long after the inception of the National Park in 1934. Back then, very few visitors drove or pulled oversized campers on the narrow winding roads. The vast majority tent camped. So when the Balsam Mountain campground was set up, builders had tent campers in mind. Today, we can camp in the fine tradition of the first park visitors.

Balsam Mountain Campground is layed out in a classic loop and sits on a rib ridge between the headwaters of Flat Creek and Bunches Creek. Past the entrance station, campsites are set along the main road.

You will immediately notice the campsites small size, a historic element of Balsam Mountain that discourages most of today's RV campers. But, even with the small sites relatively close together, you will find ample privacy, because the campground rarely fills.

> *At 5,300 feet, Balsam Mountain is Great Smoky Mountains National Park's highest campground.*

RATINGS

Beauty: ✪ ✪ ✪ ✪
Privacy: ✪ ✪ ✪
Spaciousness: ✪ ✪
Quiet: ✪ ✪ ✪ ✪
Security: ✪ ✪ ✪ ✪
Cleanliness: ✪ ✪ ✪ ✪

KEY INFORMATION

ADDRESS: Balsam Mountain Campground 107 Park Headquarters Road Gatlinburg, TN 37738

OPERATED BY: National Park Service

INFORMATION: (865) 436-1200; www.nps.gov/grsm

OPEN: Mid-May–late September

SITES: 46

EACH SITE HAS: Picnic table, fire grate

ASSIGNMENT: First come, first served; no reservations

REGISTRATION: Self-registration

FACILITIES: Water spigot, flush toilet

PARKING: At campsites only

FEE: $14 per night

ELEVATION: 5,300 feet

RESTRICTIONS: Pets: On leash only
Fires: In fire grates only
Alcohol: At campsite only
Vehicles: 30-foot trailer length limit
Other: 7-day stay limit

Keeping south on the main road, come to a loop. Campsites are spread along this loop among the fir and spruce trees. The ground slopes off steeply away from the road, resulting in some unlevel sites. With a little scouting, however, you will find a good site among the evergreens.

Balsam Mountain is off the beaten national park path. In fact, the road leading to Balsam Mountain connects to the Blue Ridge Parkway, which then connects to the main body of the National Park. There is only one trail in the nearby area, but it is a winner: Flat Creek. Leave the Heintooga Picnic Area on this path and enjoy a magnificent view of the main Smokies crest before descending to the perched watershed of Flat Creek. Cruise through an attractive, high-elevation forest before reaching the side trail to Flat Creek Falls, a steep and narrow cascade. Backtrack or continue past the falls to cross Bunches Creek and reach Balsam Mountain Road.

Balsam Mountain Road is just one of many interesting forest drives in the immediate area. Balsam Mountain Road leads 8 miles to the Blue Ridge Parkway—the granddaddy of all scenic roads in the Southern Appalachian Mountains, with recreation opportunities to both the north and south. A more rustic forest drive leaves Heintooga Picnic Area on a gravel road and runs north along Balsam Mountain before descending into Straight Fork valley to emerge at the nearby Qualla Cherokee Indian Reservation. There are several hiking trails along the way, including Palmer Creek Trail, which descends into a beautiful richly forested valley; or the Hyatt Ridge Trail, which, along with the Beech Gap Trail, makes for a rewarding high-country loop hike of 8 miles. Anglers can fish for trout on Straight Fork, or enjoy many of the stream and pond fishing opportunities on the reservation. The nearby town of Cherokee has your typical Smokies' tourist traps as well as camping supplies.

MAP

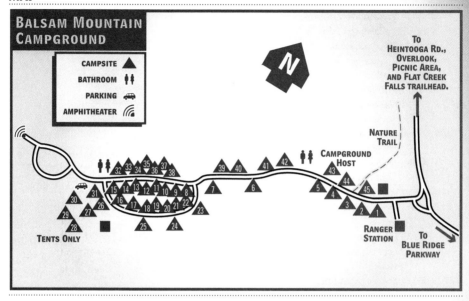

BALSAM MOUNTAIN CAMPGROUND

CAMPSITE ▲
BATHROOM
PARKING
AMPHITHEATER

To HEINTOOGA RD., OVERLOOK, PICNIC AREA, AND FLAT CREEK FALLS TRAILHEAD.

NATURE TRAIL

CAMPGROUND HOST

TENTS ONLY

RANGER STATION

To BLUE RIDGE PARKWAY

GETTING THERE

From the Oconaluftee Visitor Center near Cherokee, take Newfound Gap Road for 0.5 miles south to the Blue Ridge Parkway. Turn left onto the Blue Ridge Parkway and follow it for 10.8 miles to Heintooga Ridge Road. Turn left on Heintooga Ridge Road and drive 8 miles to Balsam Mountain campground, on your left.

BIG CREEK CAMPGROUND

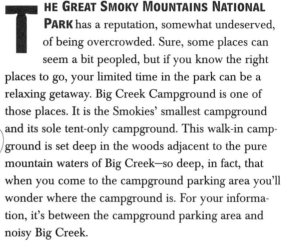

> *Only tents are allowed at this walk-in campground located in the Smokies' remote "Far East."*

THE **GREAT SMOKY MOUNTAINS NATIONAL PARK** has a reputation, somewhat undeserved, of being overcrowded. Sure, some places can seem a bit peopled, but if you know the right places to go, your limited time in the park can be a relaxing getaway. Big Creek Campground is one of those places. It is the Smokies' smallest campground and its sole tent-only campground. This walk-in campground is set deep in the woods adjacent to the pure mountain waters of Big Creek—so deep, in fact, that when you come to the campground parking area you'll wonder where the campground is. For your information, it's between the campground parking area and noisy Big Creek.

A small footpath leaves the parking area and loops the 12 campsites in the shade of tall hardwoods. Since it's a walk-in campground, you must tote your camping supplies anywhere from 100 to 300 feet. But after that, you'll be hearing only the intonations of Big Creek and smelling the wildflowers, rather than hearing an RV engine and smelling exhaust fumes.

Five of the sites are directly creekside. Each site is spacious enough to spread your gear about. The new tent pads are elevated and well drained. A somewhat sparse understory reduces privacy, but the intimate walk-in setup magnifies an atmosphere of camaraderie among fellow campers not necessarily found in larger drive-in campgrounds.

The campground comfort station borders the parking area. It houses flush toilets and a large sink with a cold-water faucet. Two other water spigots are situated along the footpath loop. A recycling bin is located in the parking area. A pay phone is located 1 mile back down the gravel road at the Big Creek Ranger Station. You can acquire limited supplies a bit farther down Big Creek at Mountain Momma's Country Store, but try to

RATINGS

Beauty: ✩ ✩ ✩ ✩
Privacy: ✩ ✩ ✩
Spaciousness: ✩ ✩ ✩ ✩ ✩
Quiet: ✩ ✩ ✩ ✩ ✩
Security: ✩ ✩ ✩ ✩
Cleanliness: ✩ ✩ ✩ ✩

bring in what you need. That way you can spend your time enjoying the park.

The Big Creek Trail starts at the campground and traces an old railroad grade from the logging era. Cool off the old-fashioned way in one of the many swimming holes that pool between the white rapids of Big Creek. Gaze up the sides of the valley; the rock bluffs you see have sheltered Smokies' wayfarers for thousands of years. Hike 3.3 miles up Big Creek and find the tumbling cascades of Mouse Creek Falls. Falls often occur where a feeder creek enters a main stream. The main stream valley erodes faster than the side stream valley, creating a hanging side canyon and then a waterfall. Continue on to Walnut Bottoms at 5 miles. This area has historically had more man–bear encounters than anywhere in the park. Keep food out of tents, and keep all food locked in your trunk when away from camp, not in the seat of your car. Crestmont Logging Company once had a camp here in the early 1900s, but now the area has returned to its former splendor. Three other trails splinter from Walnut Bottoms if you wish to explore more.

How about a strenuous hike through old-growth forest to a mountaintop capped in a Canadian-type forest with a 360-degree view from a fire tower? It's 6 miles up the Baxter Creek Trail, but your efforts will be amply rewarded. Start at the Big Creek picnic area just below the campground and go for it. Or take the Mount Sterling Trail from Mount Sterling Gap on nearby NC 284. It's only 3 miles to the tower this way. Just up from the Big Creek Ranger Station is the Chestnut Branch Trail. It leads 2 miles to the highest and wildest section of the entire Appalachian Trail, which traverses the Smoky Mountains. The historic fire tower at Mount Cammerer is only 4 miles farther. Or loop back on the Appalachian Trail to Davenport Gap and road-walk a short piece back to the campground.

Big Creek is wilderness tent camping at its best. The walk-in setting is your first step into the natural world of the Smokies. The rest of your adventure is limited only by your desire to explore the 500,000 acres in Big Creek Campground's backyard.

KEY INFORMATION

ADDRESS:	Big Creek Campground 107 Park Headquarters Road Gatlinburg, TN 37738
OPERATED BY:	Great Smoky Mountains National Park
INFORMATION:	(865) 436-1200; www.nps.gov/gsrm
OPEN:	Mid-March–October
SITES:	12
EACH SITE HAS:	Picnic table, fire pit, lantern post
ASSIGNMENT:	First come, first served; no reservations
REGISTRATION:	Self-registration
FACILITIES:	Cold water flush toilets
PARKING:	At individual sites
FEE:	$12 per night
ELEVATION:	1,700 feet
RESTRICTIONS:	Pets: On leash only Fires: In fire pits only Alcohol: At campsite only Vehicles: No RVs or trailers Other: 7-day stay limit

MAP

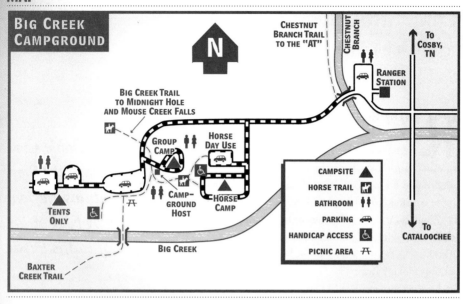

BIG CREEK CAMPGROUND

BIG CREEK TRAIL TO MIDNIGHT HOLE AND MOUSE CREEK FALLS

CHESTNUT BRANCH TRAIL TO THE "AT"

CHESTNUT BRANCH

To COSBY, TN

RANGER STATION

GROUP CAMP

HORSE DAY USE

CAMP-GROUND HOST

HORSE CAMP

TENTS ONLY

BAXTER CREEK TRAIL

BIG CREEK

To CATALOOCHEE

CAMPSITE	▲
HORSE TRAIL	
BATHROOM	
PARKING	
HANDICAP ACCESS	
PICNIC AREA	⊼

GETTING THERE

From Cove Creek take I-40 west for 15 miles, crossing the Tennessee state line, to the Waterville Exit 451. Cross the Pigeon River and turn left to follow the Pigeon upstream. Come to an intersection 2.3 miles after crossing the Pigeon. Proceed forward through the intersection and soon enter the park. Pass the Big Creek Ranger Station and drive to the end of the gravel road and the campground after 3.5 miles.

CABLE COVE CAMPGROUND

RECENT HISTORY IS A THEME of sorts for this charming and sedate campground that sits on former farmland once tilled by the Cable family. After World War II began, the demand for aluminum and the power to manufacture it soared, leading to the construction of nearby Fontana Dam. Begun in 1942, and used to generate power to produce aluminum for the war, Fontana dam remains an important source of energy. Prior to flooding behind the dam, the farming families moved away. The Forest Service moved in, later establishing a campground in the hollow.

Cable Cove's proximity to Fontana Lake makes it a favorite spot for boaters. It is an ideal camp from which to visit the Smoky Mountains via boat, thus avoiding the auto traffic. Fontana is a lightly used lake, though the views of the park are unlimited and unspoiled by troops of tourists that fill the highways on busy summer weekends.

Cable Cove Campground stretches out along a gravel road that slopes down toward Fontana Lake, half a mile away. A small loop at the end of the campground road enables drivers to turn around; this loop holds five campsites. Cable Creek, a small trout stream, parallels the road on the right. The campground is well maintained, quiet, and unassuming. Shortly after arriving, I felt as if I belonged there, like one of the neighbors.

The ten creekside sites are heavily wooded and have a thick understory. The sites are spacious, yet have an air of privacy due to the jungle-like vegetation along Cable Creek. The 11 sites opposite the creek have a glade-like grassy understory beneath second-growth trees that are reclaiming the old fields. The grass had been freshly trimmed and looked especially attractive during my stay. This "yard" space makes for a more open camping area, one conducive to visiting

> *Stay at Cable Cove and access the Smoky Mountains National Park by boat or land, free of traffic hassles.*

RATINGS

Beauty: ✿ ✿ ✿ ✿
Privacy: ✿ ✿ ✿
Spaciousness: ✿ ✿ ✿ ✿ ✿
Quiet: ✿ ✿ ✿ ✿
Security: ✿ ✿ ✿ ✿
Cleanliness: ✿ ✿ ✿ ✿ ✿

ADDRESS:	Cable Cove Campground Route 1, Box 16A Robbinsville, NC 28771
OPERATED BY:	U.S. Forest Service
INFORMATION:	(704) 479-6431; www.cs.unca.edu/nfs nc
OPEN:	April 14–October 31
SITES:	26
EACH SITE HAS:	Tent pad, lantern post, picnic table, fire grate
ASSIGNMENT:	First come, first served; no reservations
REGISTRATION:	Self-registration on site
FACILITIES:	Water, low-volume flush toilet
PARKING:	At campsites only
FEE:	$8 per night
ELEVATION:	1,800 feet
RESTRICTIONS:	**Pets:** On leash only **Fires:** In fire grates only **Alcohol:** At campsites only **Vehicles:** None **Other:** 14-day stay limit

your neighbor, a customary thing to do in friendly western North Carolina. These campsites are some of the largest I have ever seen, extending far back from the road. An area of brush and trees divides the upper and lower campground. Beyond the brush are the five sites at the turn-around loop. These sites lie beneath deep woods adjacent to Cable Creek.

Three water spigots have been placed at even intervals in the linear campground. Two comfort stations with flush toilets are at either end of the campground; campers in the middle may have to walk a bit to use them. But even this stroll could be an opportunity to get to know your neighbor. I camped toward the middle and, by the time I left, the gravel road resembled a country lane—slow-moving and full of good neighbors.

Most of your neighbors will be boaters. A high-quality boat ramp is half a mile away; campers use it to fish for bream, bass, trout, and walleye, as well as to access the National Park. Using a boat to access the park is a smart way to beat the crowds. Several hiking trails in the Smokies run right down to the lake. Check out the 360-degree view from Shuckstack Fire Tower; the tower is visible from the lake. To reach the tower, boat up the Eagle Creek arm of Fontana Lake. From the embayment, the Lost Cove Trail leads 3 miles up to the AT. Just 0.4 miles south on the AT is the tower. The outline of Fontana Lake is easily discerned from the tower. Look northeast and see the spine of the Smokies until it fades from view.

Across the water from Cable Cove is famed Hazel Creek. Its trout waters have been featured in fishing magazines for years. But don't visit just for the fish. Hike up the gentle trail that parallels the creek and discover relics of the Smokies' past, including old homesites, fields, and mining endeavors. Wide bridges spanning Hazel Creek make this walk even more pleasant. You can only access this end of the trail by boat. If you don't have a boat, contact Fontana Marina at (704) 498-2211, ext. 277, to arrange for a shuttle. The marina is only 4 miles west of Cable Cove. You can purchase limited supplies at the small store at Fontana Village Resort near the marina. But you are better off stocking up in Maryville, Tennessee, if you are coming

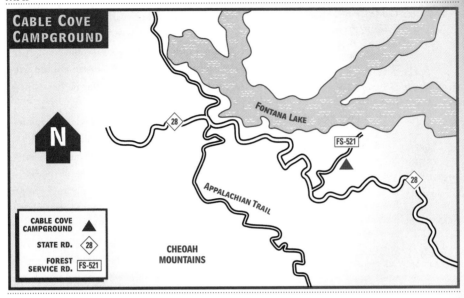

CABLE COVE CAMPGROUND

FONTANA LAKE

28

FS-521

28

APPALACHIAN TRAIL

N

CABLE COVE CAMPGROUND ▲

STATE RD. ◇ 28

FOREST SERVICE RD. FS-521

CHEOAH MOUNTAINS

from the Volunteer State, or in Robbinsville, North Carolina, south of Cable Cove on NC 143.

Also near the marina is the engineering marvel that is Fontana Dam, the tallest dam east of the Rockies at 480 feet. It is well worth a visit. A visitor center recounts the story of the dam, and cable cars take visitors down to its powerhouse. You can cross the dam in your auto, which is the landlubber's way to access the Smokies at one of the more remote trailheads. Trace the AT 3.3 miles up to Shuckstack and its tower. Or take the undulating Lakeshore Trail through the Smokies' lush flora 5 miles to Eagle Creek and its embayment. Whether by land or water, this slice of the Smokies is a gem to visit.

GETTING THERE

From Fontana Village take NC 28 east for 4.7 miles. Turn left on FS 521 for 1.5 miles. Cable Cove will be on your right.

CATALOOCHEE CAMPGROUND

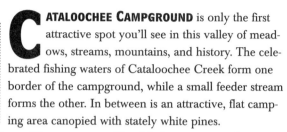

> *Cataloochee Valley's remoteness and inaccessibility make it one of the Smokies' best-kept secrets.*

CATALOOCHEE **C**AMPGROUND is only the first attractive spot you'll see in this valley of meadows, streams, mountains, and history. The celebrated fishing waters of Cataloochee Creek form one border of the campground, while a small feeder stream forms the other. In between is an attractive, flat camping area canopied with stately white pines.

The campground has ideal summer weather: warm days and cool nights. An elevation of 2,600 feet is fairly high for a valley campground with a stream the size of Cataloochee Creek. Cataloochee uses the basic campground design: campsites splintering off a loop road. Six of the sites lie along Cataloochee Creek. A few others border the small feeder stream. All the campsites are roomy and placed where the pines allow. An erratic understory of hemlock and rhododendron leaves site privacy to the luck of which site you draw. The campground host is situated at the campground's entrance for your safety and convenience. Be forewarned: Bears are sighted yearly at this campground, so properly store your food and keep the wild in the Smoky Mountain bears.

Most RV campers shy away from this campground because the park service does not recommend that RVs make the long drive over rough gravel roads. Cataloochee does fill up on summer weekends, yet with only 27 sites it doesn't seem overly crowded. A comfort station is located next to the campground at the head of the campground host. It has flush toilets and a cold-water faucet that pours into a large sink. Another water spigot is located at the other end of the campground.

With all there is to do, you probably will only be at the campground to rest from perusing the park. The first order of business is an auto tour of Cataloochee

RATINGS

Beauty: ✿ ✿ ✿ ✿ ✿
Privacy: ✿ ✿ ✿ ✿
Spaciousness: ✿ ✿ ✿ ✿ ✿
Quiet: ✿ ✿ ✿ ✿ ✿
Security: ✿ ✿ ✿ ✿
Cleanliness: ✿ ✿ ✿ ✿

Valley. Get a copy of the handy park service pamphlet at the ranger station and gain a feel of the area. An old church, a school, and numerous homesites are a delight to explore. Informative displays explain further about life long ago in this part of the world.

Cataloochee Valley is a hiker's paradise. Take the Boogerman Trail 7.4 undulating miles through different vegetation zones. The trail, which begins and ends at Caldwell Fork Trail, loops among old-growth hemlocks and tulip trees. Old homesites add a touch of human history; numerous footbridges make exploring this watery mountainland fun and easy on the feet. Or take the Little Cataloochee Trail to Little Cataloochee Church. Set in the backwoods, the church was built in 1890 and is still used today. Other signs of man you'll see are a ramshackle cabin, chimneys, fence posts, and rock walls.

The Cataloochee Divide Trail starts at 4,000 feet and rambles along the ridge line border that straddles Maggie and Cataloochee valleys. To the north is the rugged green expanse of the national park and to the south are the developed areas along US 19. Grassy knolls along the way make good viewing and relaxing spots.

Using the Rough Fork, Caldwell Fork, and Fork Ridge trails, you can make another loop, this one 9.3 miles. Pass the fields of the Woody Place, then climb Fork Ridge, descend to Caldwell Fork, and climb Fork Ridge yet again to experience the literal highs and lows of Appalachian hiking.

The meadows of Cataloochee Valley are an ideal setting for a picnic. Decide on your favorite view and lay down your blanket. Nearby shady streams will serenade you as you look up at the wooded ridges that line the valley. Deer and other critters feed at the edges of the fields. Dusk is an ideal time to see Cataloochee's wildlife.

During our last stay at this campground, summer weather had finally hit during our campground venture. The air had a lazy, hazy feel as we toured the valley's historic structures. I fished away the afternoon, catching and releasing a few rainbows downstream

KEY INFORMATION

ADDRESS:	Cataloochee Campground 107 Park Headquarters Road Gatlinburg, TN 37738
OPERATED BY:	Great Smoky Mountains National Park
INFORMATION:	(865) 436-1200; www.nps.gov/grsm
OPEN:	Mid-March–October
SITES:	27
EACH SITE HAS:	Picnic table, fire pit, lantern post
ASSIGNMENT:	First come, first served; no reservations
REGISTRATION:	Self-registration on site
FACILITIES:	Cold water, flush toilets
PARKING:	At individual sites
FEE:	$12 per night
ELEVATION:	2,610 feet
RESTRICTIONS:	Pets: On leash only Fires: In fire pits only Alcohol: At campsites only Vehicles: None Other: 7-day stay limit

MAP

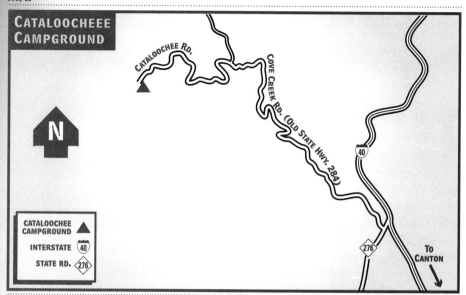

CATALOOCHEEE CAMPGROUND

CATALOOCHEE RD.

COVE CREEK RD. (OLD STATE HWY. 284)

N

40

CATALOOCHEE CAMPGROUND	▲
INTERSTATE	40
STATE RD.	276

276

To CANTON

GETTING THERE

From Canton drive 11 miles west on I-40 to Exit 20, then drive west on NC 276. Follow it a short distance, then turn right on Cove Creek Road, which you follow nearly 6 miles to enter the park. Two miles beyond the park boundary, turn left onto the paved Cataloochee Road and follow it 3 miles. The campground will be on your left.

from the campground. After grilling hamburgers for supper, we walked up the Rough Fork Trail to the Woody Place. The homestead looked picturesque as the late-evening sunlight filtered through the nearby forest. As we came back to the trailhead, deer browsed in the Cataloochee meadow. We knew we had come to the right place. So will you.

DOUGHTON CAMPGROUND

THE **NATIONAL PARK SERVICE** does a really good job with this Blue Ridge Parkway campground. It is located on the crest of the Blue Ridge and has a mountaintop ambience. A smart design spreads out 100-plus sites and makes the area seem like several small campgrounds. Dividing the tent and RV sites into separate sections makes it even better.

The 6,430-acre park and campground are named after former North Carolina Congressman "Muley Bob" Doughton, who fought hard to make the Parkway become the scenic reality it is. He would be proud of this area, which unobtrusively integrates modern structures into the historic dwellings and hiking trails that lace the park.

Before you explore Doughton Park, pick a campsite. That may take a few minutes, as Doughton Campground has six distinct camping areas. It is a generally open, airy campground that is tastefully landscaped and well integrated into the ridge top setting. Even the most discriminating tent campers will find a site to suit their tastes.

The first loop holds 22 sites and is heavily wooded, yet with a light understory. The sites undulate along a hill and are fairly close, so you may be a tad close to your neighbor. The comfort station is a ways down a sloping path, possibly a little farther than some are willing to walk.

Sites 23–33 are set back in the woods, down from the paved campground road. Short paths lead back to these sites, so you will have to carry your gear to your site. This distance allows for the most rustic camping experience, out of sight from vehicles. The sites closest to the parking area border a grassy field adjacent to the parking area. Campers share the comfort station with the first loop via a short, paved path.

> *Doughton Campground is much more than a way station along the Blue Ridge Parkway.*

RATINGS

Beauty: ✿ ✿ ✿ ✿
Privacy: ✿ ✿ ✿
Spaciousness: ✿ ✿ ✿
Quiet: ✿ ✿ ✿
Security: ✿ ✿ ✿ ✿
Cleanliness: ✿ ✿ ✿ ✿ ✿

KEY INFORMATION

ADDRESS: Doughton Campground
199 Hamphill Knob Road
Asheville, NC 28801

OPERATED BY: National Park Service

INFORMATION: (828) 298-0398;
www.nps.gov/blri

OPEN: May–October

SITES: 135 tent and RV sites

EACH SITE HAS: Tent pad, fire ring, picnic table

ASSIGNMENT: First come, first served; no reservations

REGISTRATION: At campground hut

FACILITIES: Water flush toilets, pay phone

PARKING: At campsites only

FEE: $12 per night

ELEVATION: 3,600 feet

RESTRICTIONS: Pets: On 6-foot or shorter leash
Fires: In fire rings only
Alcohol: At campsites only
Vehicles: None
Other: 14-day stay limit, 30-day total limit for calendar year

The second loop circles the highest point of the campground. It has 30 sites and is centered with a grassy glade where a water tank sits. Oddly enough, a campsite is located right by the water tank. When I checked it out, I found the view of the surrounding mountain lands worth the intrusion of the green structure. Other sites up there offer intermittent views of the Blue Ridge and beyond. You even have a view from the comfort station at the loop's center.

The main loop continues along the ridge and passes a few sites for larger pop-up tent campers, then enters the campfire circle loop. It has nine sites located in an attractive meadow. Trees have been strategically planted by each campsite for shade and aesthetic appeal.

Beyond the campfire circle loop is yet another loop winding amid hilly forestland. This loop rolls and dips between rock outcrops, with sites tastefully integrated where the land allows. There are 20 sites here. Since it is at the very back of the campground, you will have the least amount of vehicles casually driving by to their respective sites. A comfort station is centered on this loop as well.

Back on the main loop, in an open area backed against woodland, are 11 more sites for larger pop-ups. For such a large campground, there is a curious lack of faucets; there are only six and they could have been better placed. But this is a minor inconvenience for this well-kept and secure campground that is 90% tent campers. A campground host lives on site.

The Blue Ridge Parkway is an exercise in scenic beauty, but I think this particular area is exceptional even for the BRP. A drive in either direction will sate your taste for dramatic landscapes and historic sites. The Brinegar Cabin is just a short distance north. Of course, the most rewarding views are those earned with a little sweat.

Doughton Park has over 30 miles of trails that meander through pastures, along wooded ridges, and by mountain streams. The Bluff Mountain Trail departs from the campground and gives you a sampling of this country. It extends for 3 or so miles in each direction.

MAP

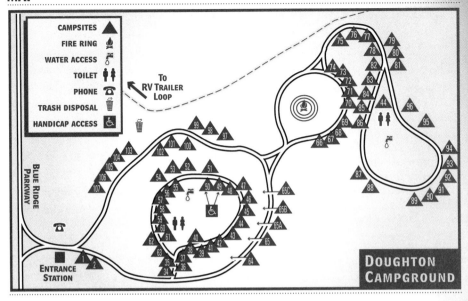

Legend

- CAMPSITES ▲
- FIRE RING
- WATER ACCESS
- TOILET
- PHONE
- TRASH DISPOSAL
- HANDICAP ACCESS

To RV TRAILER LOOP

BLUE RIDGE PARKWAY

ENTRANCE STATION

DOUGHTON CAMPGROUND

The Fodderstack Trail climbs to the Wildcat Rocks Overlook and is a 2-mile round-trip. Another recommended trail is Basin Creek, which ends at the Caudill Cabin. This cabin is only accessible by foot. Cedar Ridge Trail begins at the Brinegar Cabin and drops down to Basin Creek. Before you hike any of these trails, stop at the campground hut and pick up a free trail map. Get out there and stretch your legs after enjoying that fantastic Blue Ridge Parkway scenery.

GETTING THERE

Take NC 18 west from Sparta for 14 miles to the Blue Ridge Parkway. Turn north on the Parkway, drive 6 miles to milepost 239. Doughton Park Campground will be on your left.

HANGING DOG
CAMPGROUND

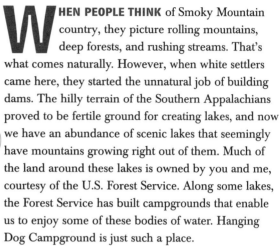

> *Hanging Dog sits by picturesque Hiwassee Lake, nestled in the rural mountains of western North Carolina.*

WHEN PEOPLE THINK of Smoky Mountain country, they picture rolling mountains, deep forests, and rushing streams. That's what comes naturally. However, when white settlers came here, they started the unnatural job of building dams. The hilly terrain of the Southern Appalachians proved to be fertile ground for creating lakes, and now we have an abundance of scenic lakes that seemingly have mountains growing right out of them. Much of the land around these lakes is owned by you and me, courtesy of the U.S. Forest Service. Along some lakes, the Forest Service has built campgrounds that enable us to enjoy some of these bodies of water. Hanging Dog Campground is just such a place.

Hanging Dog is an unusual name for a campground. It is named after a nearby creek of the same name that flows through a parcel of the neighboring Cherokee Reservation. Legend has it that a brave dog was accidentally snared in the creek while chasing a deer to provide meat for the hungry people. The dog survived and the people named the area to commemorate the canine's actions.

Hanging Dog Campground features four widely separated loops. Each loop is almost like its own campground. A dry pine-oak forest covers the peninsula that borders Hiwassee Lake. Adequate, yet sparse, water supplies and comfort stations are placed in every loop.

This Civilian Conservation Corps–era campground has aged well. Vegetation cultivated over many decades provides ideal campground aesthetics, and in this relaxed atmosphere time seems to move slowly. Adults, who first visited Hanging Dog as children, pass on the joys of camping here to the next generation.

Loop A spurs off to the right of the campground's main road and circles a hollow formed by a tiny

RATINGS

Beauty: ✩ ✩ ✩ ✩
Privacy: ✩ ✩ ✩ ✩
Spaciousness: ✩ ✩ ✩ ✩ ✩
Quiet: ✩ ✩ ✩
Security: ✩ ✩ ✩ ✩
Cleanliness: ✩ ✩ ✩ ✩

stream. The lower reaches of the loop are piney and open. The vegetation thickens farther up the hollow, allowing more site privacy. The campsites are well established and spacious. Landscaping timbers have been strategically placed to help with site leveling and delineation.

Loop B forms a figure eight along an arm of Hiwassee Lake. The 15 sites there are located in a grassy glade beneath tall pines. The five most popular campsites in this loop fit snugly against the lake.

Pass over quite a few speed bumps and reach Loop C. It also forms a crude figure eight and is a long walk down the main campground road from the first two loops. Enter an open pine forest with spacious campsites. The backside of the loop runs along a small rhododendron-choked branch that provides a more dense understory and increased site privacy.

Loop D is located across the road from Loop C and is situated in some rolling woods. It offers the most densely forested sites, with a thick understory of mountain laurel and small trees. The loop is now used as a picnic area and for overflow camping when all the other sites are taken, which is a shame because it's the most attractive loop.

The 180 miles of picturesque, wooded shoreline of Hiwassee Lake are primarily under Forest Service stewardship, minimizing development. Bass, bream, and crappie are among the species that provide excellent fishing in these mountain lakes. The transparent, green waters will lure you in for a swim on a hot summer day. Boaters can access the lake at the boat ramp at the very end of the main campground road.

Two hiking trails meander from the campground around the peninsula. The Mingus Trail starts across from Loop B and runs through pine-oak woods down to the boat ramp, where you can return to your campsite on the road. The Ramsey Bluff Trail starts at the back of Loop B and winds along the shore of Hiwassee Lake for 2.2 miles and ends at the back of Loop D.

The nearby town of Murphy is worth more than just a supply run. It is a quintessentially quaint town. Absorb the ambience, and make certain you visit the

ADDRESS:	Hanging Dog Campground 201 Woodland Drive Murphy, NC 28906
OPERATED BY:	U.S. Forest Service
INFORMATION:	(828) 837-5152; www.cs.unca.edu/nfsnc
OPEN:	May–October
SITES:	67
EACH SITE HAS:	Tent pad, fire ring, picnic table, lantern post
ASSIGNMENT:	First come, first served; no reservations
REGISTRATION:	Self-registration on site
FACILITIES:	Water, flush toilets
PARKING:	At campsites only
FEE:	$8 per night
ELEVATION:	1,600 feet
RESTRICTIONS:	**Pets:** On 6-foot or shorter leash **Fires:** In fire rings only **Alcohol:** At campsites only **Vehicles:** At campsites only **Other:** 14-day stay limit; after a 7 day absence one is allowed to return

MAP

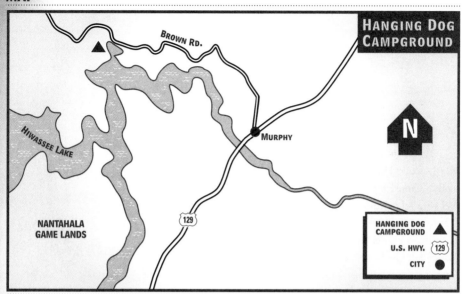

GETTING THERE

From Murphy take Brown Road (NC 1326) NW for 5 miles. Turn left at campground sign. Hanging Dog will be straight ahead.

Cherokee County Historical Society Museum. You can see what life was like in the pre-industrial era. You'll find that much of the good from that bygone era is still alive today in this slice of Americana.

HORSE COVE
CAMPGROUND

Robbinsville

HORSE COVE IS AN UNPRETENTIOUS, small campground adjacent to playful Santeetlah (pronounced San-TEE-lah) Creek. Located primarily along Horse Cove Branch, a tributary of Santeetlah Creek, Horse Cove has an unpolished, old-time feel with its minimal facilities. In a way, it is two campgrounds: the lower 6, year-round sites and the upper 11, warm-weather sites. The lower, year-round sites on Santeetlah Creek are across Forest Service Road 416 from the main campground. They have a spur road of their own. A pit toilet is the only amenity, although water is available from a spigot in summer and the creek in winter. These sites overlook Santeetlah Creek from a heavily wooded knoll.

The upper campground runs up a narrow valley carved by Horse Cove Branch, which forms the western campground border. A steep mountainside hems in the campground to the east, but the campsites are graded and kept level with landscaping timbers. This hillside arrangement spreads campsites apart both horizontally and vertically. A comfort station with low-flow, flush toilets is located at the campground entrance. You're never far from one of the three water spigots that are conveniently placed about this cozy encampment.

A spare, gravel road divides the upper campground. Beneath a hardwood canopy, the five sites beyond Horse Cove Branch are open and dry. They are well spaced along the road, which makes a short loop. The grassy center of the loop has a horseshoe pit. The six campsites adjacent to boisterous Horse Cove Branch are isolated from each other by large rocks intermingled with rhododendron and hemlock. The Horse Cove Trail leads to the high country right from the upper campground, but then ends and splits into

> *Stay at Horse Cove Campground and enjo the lovely trees of Joyce Kilmer Memorial Forest and the Slickrock Wilderness.*

RATINGS

Beauty: ✿ ✿ ✿ ✿
Privacy: ✿ ✿ ✿ ✿
Spaciousness: ✿ ✿ ✿ ✿ ✿
Quiet: ✿ ✿ ✿ ✿
Security: ✿ ✿ ✿ ✿
Cleanliness: ✿ ✿ ✿ ✿

ADDRESS: Horse Cove Campground
Route 1, Box 16-A
Robbinsville, NC 28771

OPERATED BY: U.S. Forest Service

INFORMATION: (828) 479-6431;
www.cs.unca.edu/nfs nc

OPEN: Upper campground, April 15–October 31; lower campground, year-round

SITES: 26

EACH SITE HAS: Tent pad, fire grate, picnic table, lantern post

ASSIGNMENT: First come, first served; no reservations

REGISTRATION: Self-registration on site

FACILITIES: Water in summer, flush toilets in summer, vault toilets in winter

PARKING: At individual sites

FEE: $8 per night, April through October; $5 in winter

ELEVATION: 2,300 feet

RESTRICTIONS: **Pets:** On leash only
Fires: In fire grates only
Alcohol: At campsites only
Vehicles: None
Other: 14-day stay limit

two trails along divergent railroad grades remaining from the logging days.

Horse Cove is a nice campground, but the reason for its existence is its proximity to the magnificent Joyce Kilmer Memorial Forest and the adjoining Slickrock Wilderness. Hikers love to walk among the giants of this forest, named for the late writer Joyce Kilmer. He met an untimely end in France during World War I on July 30, 1918. This accomplished author penned a famous poem entitled "Trees." The first two lines of this poem are: "I think that I shall never see/A poem as lovely as a tree."

After his death, a nationwide search ensued to locate a forest grand enough to memorialize Kilmer. Finally, a tract in North Carolina was selected. What we see today is a 3,800-acre, old-growth woodland that is one of the most impressive remnants of what the Southern Appalachians looked like before the loggers permanently altered the landscape.

Several trails start at the Joyce Kilmer Memorial Forest parking area, which is 0.7 miles west of the Horse Cove Campground on FS 416. The Joyce Kilmer National Recreation Trail forms a figure eight as it loops through the forest. The 0.8-mile upper loop that travels through Poplar Cove is said to have the densest concentration of large trees in eastern North America. Tulip trees, 20 feet around the base, rise to meet the sun alongside their fellow forest dwellers: hemlock, beech, and oak. The largest cucumber tree in North Carolina is marked with a plaque.

You can't go wrong with any of the three trails that lead out of Joyce Kilmer Memorial Forest into the high country of the Joyce Kilmer–Slickrock Wilderness. A loop hike of differing combinations is possible using any of the Stratton Bald, Naked Ground, and Jenkins Meadow/Hangover Lead trails. For a scenic blockbuster of a hike, take the old Cherokee trading path, known to modern hikers as the Naked Ground Trail. It climbs 4.3 miles to Naked Ground, named for its lack of trees in days gone by. To your left, it is 1.3 miles to Bob Stratton Bald, a mile-high mountain meadow with rewarding views of the Smoky and Nantahala forests. When cattle grazing ceased here, the

MAP

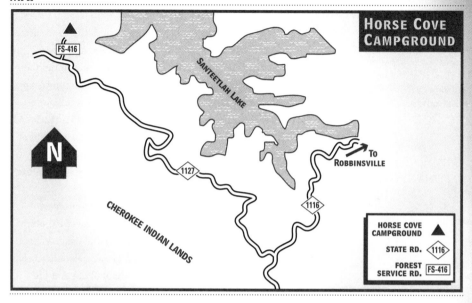

HORSE COVE CAMPGROUND

SANTEETLAH LAKE

FS-416

N

1127

1116

To ROBBINSVILLE

CHEROKEE INDIAN LANDS

HORSE COVE CAMPGROUND	▲
STATE RD.	◁1116▷
FOREST SERVICE RD.	FS-416

field began to reforest. In the late 1980s, however, trees were cut back and native grasses were planted. Consequently, the meadow and its beautiful views were restored. It's my favorite place in this wilderness.

From Naked Ground, it is 1.4 miles (right) to Hangover Lead. This sheer, rocky drop-off needs no assistance from the Forest Service to maintain its views. The Smoky Mountains and Gregory Bald's open field are visible to your right. The lakes and mountains that are the legacy of western North Carolina and eastern Tennessee are all around you. Return via the Naked Ground or Hangover Lead trails.

GETTING THERE

From Robbinsville take US 129 north for 1 mile, then turn left on NC 143. Go 3.5 miles to NC 1127 and turn right. Go 12 miles to FS 416 and turn right; FS 416 soon bisects the campground.

LAKE JAMES
STATE PARK

> *All the sites here are walk-in and most are directly on Lake James!*

LAKE JAMES IS ONE of the cleanest, clearest lakes in the Carolinas. It also has some of the best views, as the high mountains of the Pisgah National Forest burst skyward beyond the water to the northwest. The fine waters of the Pisgah feed Lake James. The contemporary facilities reflect the park being one of North Carolina's newer public preserves.

The sign for Lake James State Park on I-40 says, "No RV Camping." I knew then it was a likely inclusion for this book. It's a good thing all the turns between the interstate and the state park were signed, otherwise finding the park would have been very difficult. The campground exceeded adequate and is actually ideal for tent campers. The nice bathhouse and two disabled-access campsites, campsites 19 and 20, are immediately adjacent to the walk-in parking area. A hilltop field backs the parking area, and a foot trail leads to the balance of the campsites.

The foot trail leads toward Lake James. Tulip trees and other hardwoods shade the peninsula jutting into the deeply colored water. Reach campsites 1, 2, and 3. These are on the perimeter of a small knob where the campground wood yard stands. Pine and locust trees shade these sites, two of which are cut into a hill.

Another trail circles down to the lake and the lakeside campsites. Campsite 4 is on a point overlooking the lake. Shortoff Mountain and Table Rock Mountain are easily visible in the distance. A wood fence borders the campsite along the lake, as it is a good 20 feet off a bluff down to the water. A walking trail continues to the rest of the campsites. Campsite 5 is long and narrow. Campsite 6 overlooks the lake and is shaded by pines. Campsite 7 is on the small side. Campsite 8 is highly coveted for its great views. Campsite 9 is 30 feet back from the lake and is cut into the mountainside. Campsite 10 has numerous landscaping

RATINGS

Beauty: ✪ ✪ ✪ ✪ ✪
Privacy: ✪ ✪ ✪
Spaciousness: ✪ ✪ ✪
Quiet: ✪ ✪ ✪
Security: ✪ ✪ ✪ ✪ ✪
Cleanliness: ✪ ✪ ✪ ✪ ✪

timbers that tier down to the lake itself, where a tiny beach overlooks a cove. Campsite 11 is back from the water a bit. Campsite 12 is directly on the cove. Campsite 13 is smallish and shaded by white pines. Campsite 14 is close to site 13. The water laps up to campsite 15. Campsite 16 is in a small flat. Campsite 17 is near an old foundation with steps leading to the lake. Campsite 18 is ideal for solitude seekers. It is back in the woods all by itself with a path leading to it and it alone.

Water spigots are adequately spaced throughout the area with few sites spaced over a large area. Trails lead back toward the campground bathhouse. This campground will fill during good weather weekends during late spring until Labor Day. Sites are available during the week anytime the campground is open.

Many campers use this as a base camp to explore western North Carolina, from Linville Gorge and the Blue Ridge Parkway to Asheville and the Biltmore Hotel. Other campers remain within the confines of the park. Others just hang around their campsite. These *are* good campsites.

Lake James is 6,510 acres of alluring water and has 150 miles of shoreline. The state park has 5 miles of shoreline. The swim beach is popular with tent campers during the summer. Expect the aqua to be a tad cooler than your average lake. Canoes are available for rent during the summer.

Those with boats will be launching at one of two nearby boat ramps to explore a few acres of water and a few miles of shoreline. The cool deep waters harbor largemouth bass, smallmouth bass, bream, and walleye. Hiking trails are a bit limited at this small state park. One trail leads half a mile to Sandy Cliff Overlook, where you can enjoy more of those lake and mountain vistas. A 1.5-mile path leads from the campground to Lake Channel Overlook. The Fox Den Trail is the park's longest at 2.2 miles. An information board at the walk-in parking area will get you oriented. Hopefully, you will orient yourself and your tent to the lake-view, walk-in tent sites at Lake James State Park.

KEY INFORMATION

ADDRESS: Lake James State Park
P.O. Box 340
Nebo, NC 28761

OPERATED BY: North Carolina State Park

INFORMATION: (828) 652-5047; www.ncsparks.net

OPEN: March 15 through November 30

SITES: 20

EACH SITE HAS: Picnic table, fire ring, lantern post, tent pad

ASSIGNMENT: First come, first served; no reservations

REGISTRATION: Ranger will come by and register you

FACILITIES: Hot showers, water spigots

PARKING: At walk-in tent parking only

FEE: $12 per night

ELEVATION: 1,240 feet

RESTRICTIONS: **Pets:** On leash only
Fires: In fire rings only
Alcohol: Prohibited
Vehicles: None
Other: 14-day stay limit

MAP

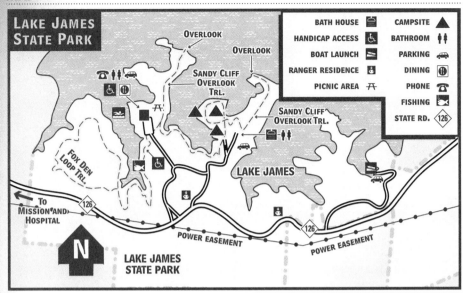

LAKE JAMES STATE PARK

OVERLOOK

OVERLOOK

SANDY CLIFF OVERLOOK TRL.

SANDY CLIFF OVERLOOK TRL.

Fox Den Loop Trl.

LAKE JAMES

To MISSION AND HOSPITAL

126

POWER EASEMENT

POWER EASEMENT

126

N

LAKE JAMES STATE PARK

BATH HOUSE		CAMPSITE		
HANDICAP ACCESS		BATHROOM		
BOAT LAUNCH		PARKING		
RANGER RESIDENCE		DINING		
PICNIC AREA		PHONE		
		FISHING		
		STATE RD.	126	

GETTING THERE

From Exit 90 on I-40 west of Morganton, leave north from the interstate, taking Fairview Road for 0.4 miles to Harmony Grove Road. Turn right on Harmony Grove Road and follow it for 2.1 miles to reach US 70. Turn left on US 70 west and follow it 0.2 miles to reach NC 126 east. Turn right on NC 126 east and follow it 2.7 miles to the state park, on your left.

LINVILLE FALLS CAMPGROUND

THE **BLUE RIDGE PARKWAY** is an unusual national park. It is linear, stretching 469 miles on the spine of the Southern Appalachians, connecting Great Smoky Mountain and Shenandoah national parks. When deciding to designate the first national park in our southern mountains, government officials just couldn't decide between Shenandoah and the Smokies, so both were developed. As a result of this compromise the scenic road connecting them was built. In the process, officials brought many historic sites and attractive natural features under the park service umbrella. One of these outstanding areas is Linville Falls, the crown jewel of Linville Gorge, which many feel to be the most scenic wilderness in the Tar Heel State.

Linville Falls has a campground just off the parkway that can be your base camp for exploring Linville Gorge. With 70 sites, this campground is fairly large. Fifty of the seventy sites are for tent campers. Oddly, the tent and trailer sites are intermixed along two paved camping loops with paved pull-ins. The setting, at 3,200 feet in elevation, is a flat alongside Linville River. A mixture of white pine, hardwoods, rhododendron, and open grassy areas allows campers to choose the amount of sun and shade they want. Along Loop A, there are several appealing tent sites set in the woods directly alongside the clean, clear Linville River.

On the B Loop, there are two groupings of tent sites beneath beech trees. Your best bet is to cruise the loops and look for the tent sites that appeal to you. A sizable grassy meadow is free of campsites and makes for a great sunning or relaxing spot. The biggest drawback to the campground is its mixed placement of tent and trailer campsites. Nonetheless, choosy tent campers will be able to find a quality spot. Water spigots are scattered about the campground, and the two

> *Linville Falls lies at the head of the rugged Linville Gorge Wilderness.*

RATINGS

Beauty: ☆ ☆ ☆
Privacy: ☆ ☆ ☆
Spaciousness: ☆ ☆ ☆ ☆
Quiet: ☆ ☆ ☆
Security: ☆ ☆ ☆ ☆ ☆
Cleanliness: ☆ ☆ ☆ ☆ ☆

ADDRESS:	Linville Falls Campground 199 Hemphill Knob Road Asheville, NC 28801
OPERATED BY:	National Park Service
INFORMATION:	(704) 298-0398; www.nps.gov/blri
OPEN:	Year-round
SITES:	50 tent sites, 70 total
EACH SITE HAS:	Picnic table, fire grate, grill
ASSIGNMENT:	First come, first served; no reservations
REGISTRATION:	At campground entrance booth
FACILITIES:	Water spigot (May–October), flush toilets
PARKING:	At campsites only
FEE:	$12 per night
ELEVATION:	3,200 feet
RESTRICTIONS:	Pets: On 6-foot or shorter leash Fires: In fire grates only Alcohol: At campsites only Vehicles: 30-foot trailer length Other: 14-day stay limit, 30 days per year

bathroom facilities are located within easy walking distance of all the campsites. For your safety and convenience campground hosts and park personnel are on-site in the warm season. During winter, the water is turned off and vault toilets are used.

Linville Falls is your mandatory first destination. The falls, in two sections, drops at the point where the Linville River descends into its famous gorge. A park visitor center near the campground is your departure point. The Erwins View Trail is a 1.6-mile round-trip taking hikers by four overlooks, passing the upper and lower falls. The Upper Falls View comes first. You can see both falls from Chimney View. The Gorge View allows a look down into the deep swath cut by the Linville River as it descends between Linville Mountain and Jonas Ridge. Erwins View offers an even more expansive vista than the previous three views. Another hike leads steeply from the visitor center down to the Plunge Basin, at the base of the falls. To access the main gorge, managed under the auspices of the U.S. Forest Service, campers must drive a short distance to Wisemans View Road and the Kistler Memorial Highway, which is a scenic auto destination rivaling the Blue Ridge Parkway. Below, the Linville Gorge Wilderness covers nearly 11,000 acres. Wisemans View is particularly scenic, allowing visitors to gaze up the gorge. Hikers have to trace steep and challenging trails to reach the river down in the gorge. A trail map of the gorge is available at the parkway visitor center. Bynum Bluff Trail makes a sharp drop down to a sharp bend in the river. Babel Tower Trail ends at a locale encircled by the Linville River on three sides. Before taking off on any of these trails you might want to get a hearty meal at the nearby Linville Falls community, where you can also buy limited camping supplies.

MAP

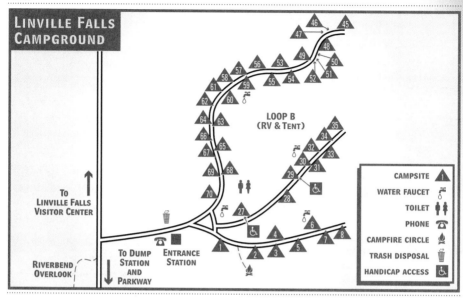

LINVILLE FALLS CAMPGROUND

LOOP B
(RV & TENT)

TO
LINVILLE FALLS
VISITOR CENTER

RIVERBEND
OVERLOOK

TO DUMP
STATION
AND
PARKWAY

ENTRANCE
STATION

CAMPSITE	▲
WATER FAUCET	⌐
TOILET	♟♟
PHONE	☎
CAMPFIRE CIRCLE	♨
TRASH DISPOSAL	🗑
HANDICAP ACCESS	♿

GETTING THERE

From Spruce Pine, drive east on NC 226 for 6 miles to the Blue Ridge Parkway. Head north on the Blue Ridge Parkway for 12 miles to milepost 316.3 and Linville Falls. The campground will be on the right.

MOUNT MITCHELL
STATE PARK

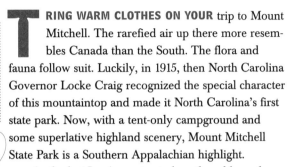

> *Mount Mitchell is the highest point in the eastern United States and has the highest tent-only campground.*

TRING WARM CLOTHES ON YOUR trip to Mount Mitchell. The rarefied air up there more resembles Canada than the South. The flora and fauna follow suit. Luckily, in 1915, then North Carolina Governor Locke Craig recognized the special character of this mountaintop and made it North Carolina's first state park. Now, with a tent-only campground and some superlative highland scenery, Mount Mitchell State Park is a Southern Appalachian highlight.

As the last Ice Age retreated north, cold-weather plants and animals of the north retreated with them—except for those that survived on the highest peaks down in Dixie. These mountaintops formed, in effect, cool-climate islands where the northern species continue to survive. Unfortunately, the mountaintop is under siege by acid rain, insect pests, and a severe climate. As a result, some trees and plants are dying.

Mount Mitchell's campground is for tents only, unless you can carry an RV from the parking area up the stone steps to the campground. The short walk immediately enters the dense forest once dominated by the Fraser fir. Today, stunted and weather-beaten mountain ash and a few other hardwoods mingle with the firs. Dead trees remind you of the trouble these forests face.

The nine campsites splinter off the gravel path that rises with the mountainside. They are set into the land amid the dense woods. The sites are small and fairly close together, but are private due to the heavy plant growth. There is little canopy overhead, as the trees become gnarled the higher they grow. There are two water spigots along the short path. A bathroom with flush toilets is midway along the path. Firewood is for sale at $3 per bundle in the parking area.

Sites 1 and 9 are the most private, but feel lucky to get a site at all during summer weekends. With only

RATINGS

Beauty: ✩ ✩ ✩ ✩ ✩
Site privacy: ✩ ✩ ✩ ✩
Spaciousness: ✩ ✩ ✩
Quiet: ✩ ✩ ✩ ✩
Security: ✩ ✩ ✩ ✩ ✩
Cleanliness: ✩ ✩ ✩ ✩ ✩

nine sites, this tiny campground exudes an intimate, secluded feel. The only noise you'll hear is the wind whipping over your head. By the way, Mount Mitchell is covered in fog, rain, or snow eight out of ten days per year. Snow has been recorded every month of the year. Annually it receives 104 inches of snow. Don't let those facts deter you; weather is part of the phenomenon that is Mount Mitchell.

The fog rolled in and out of the campground during our midsummer trip. Now and then the sun would shine, warming us. Wooded ridges came in and out of view with the fog; the whole scene seemed like some other world.

Carry a jacket along when you tramp the park. First drive up to the summit parking area and make the short jaunt to the observation tower atop Mount Mitchell. There lies the remains of Elisha Mitchell, who fell to his death from a waterfall after measuring the height of the mountain. From the tower you can see the Black Mountain Range and beyond. Back near the parking area, check out the museum that details the natural history of Mount Mitchell.

Many hiking trails thread the park. From the campground you can walk to the observation tower and connect to the Deep Gap Trail; it's a rugged 6-mile hike along the Black Mountain Range to several peaks that stand over 6,000 feet in elevation. Or you can leave the campground on the Old Mount Mitchell Trail past the park restaurant and loop around Mount Hallback to return to the campground.

Mount Mitchell State Park is surrounded by the Pisgah National Forest, which is bisected by the Blue Ridge Parkway. This, in essence, increases the accessible forest area beyond the 1,860-acre state park. Many national forest trails connect to the state park trails, allowing nearly unlimited hiking opportunities. Procure a trail map from the park office for the best hiking experience.

Get your supplies in Asheville before you leave. The Blue Ridge Parkway makes for a scenic drive, but once in the highlands of the Black Mountains, you won't want to leave this wonderful mountaintop and campground.

MAP

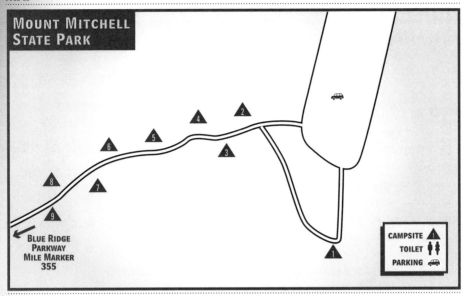

MOUNT MITCHELL STATE PARK

BLUE RIDGE
PARKWAY
MILE MARKER
355

CAMPSITE	▲
TOILET	👫
PARKING	🚗

GETTING THERE

From Asheville take the Blue Ridge Parkway north for 34 miles to milepost 355. Turn left into Mount Mitchell State Park. The campground is 4 miles up the road on your right.

NELSON'S NANTAHALA HIDEAWAY CAMPGROUND

THE OWNERS OF THIS FACILITY knew they had a good location for tent campers to access the numerous outdoor features in the immediate vicinity, so they set about creating a quality campground to match the first-rate scenery of the area. They're still working out a few kinks, but you will be more than satisfied with your stay here.

Pass the campground office, which has ice and soft-drink machines, and enter the campground. The campground design features the classic loop, which climbs up the side of a hill along a small creek, Powder Burnt Branch. The campsites are set along tiers that extend from one side of the loop to the other. Because of the tiers, campers enjoy topographic relief yet don't have to camp on a slope, as the tiers are level and evenly graded. The lower end of the loop is more open.

Several generations ago the campground was a cornfield. Later, trees reclaimed the site. When the campground was built, the many trees were left to flourish and naturally landscape Nelson's Hideaway. Tree cover thickens as the campground rises, and a thick carpet of grass forms the campground understory.

Water spigots are spread throughout the campground. The centrally located bathhouse is simply the finest I've ever seen this side of a fancy hotel, much less a campground. Divided by gender, each attractive section contains three hot showers and flush toilets inside a rustic, wood exterior. You can wash your dirty duds at the laundry facility, located here as well.

If you don't feel like pitching your tent, use one of the Adirondack-style, open-air shelters at the beginning of the loop. They have padded bunks and a small porch to enjoy the cool mountain breezes. The shelters have a picnic table beside them too. Three sizable group campsites are located in a flat across Powder Burnt Branch. They can be reached by crossing a small footbridge.

> *This campground offers easy access to the Nantahala River Gorge and numerous biking and hiking trails.*

RATINGS

Beauty: ✿ ✿ ✿
Privacy: ✿ ✿ ✿
Spaciousness: ✿ ✿ ✿ ✿
Quiet: ✿ ✿ ✿ ✿
Security: ✿ ✿ ✿ ✿ ✿
Cleanliness: ✿ ✿ ✿ ✿ ✿

KEY INFORMATION

ADDRESS: Nelson's Nantahala Hideaway Campground P.O. Box 25, US 19/74 Topton, NC 28781

OPERATED BY: Jimmy Kyle Davis

INFORMATION: (828) 321-4407

OPEN: Mid-April–October

SITES: 30

EACH SITE HAS: Tent area, picnic table, fire ring

ASSIGNMENT: By reservation or first come, first served

REGISTRATION: At campground office; reserve by phone (800) 936-6649

FACILITIES: Water, hot showers, laundry, soft-drink machine, some electrical hookups

PARKING: At campsites only

FEE: $12 per night for 2 people; $2 each additional person

ELEVATION: 2,800 feet

RESTRICTIONS: **Pets:** On leash only **Fires:** In fire rings only **Alcohol:** At campsites only **Vehicles:** None

Tent campers seek out the top of the loop, where the woods thicken and campers are kings of the hill. There, campers can see across the valley to the Snowbird Mountains.

The middle tiers of the campground are equipped with electricity in addition to the regular amenities. But don't expect too many RVs here. It's a steep climb to the campground from the highway. In addition, with all the hiking, canoeing, and kayaking opportunities, active campers are likely to be found here.

Just 2 miles north is the Nantahala River Launch Site. There, canoers and kayakers enter the river gorge for a 9-mile run of nationally known whitewater floating. Commercial outfitters will accommodate inexperienced thrill seekers who long to challenge the chilly, continuous rapids.

The Nelson family has built hiking trails on its land that connect to the Apple Tree national forest trails that border the campground. This is only fitting, since earlier family generations actually sold the Apple Tree land to the federal government to form a section of the Nantahala National Forest. These forest trails follow old Cherokee routes that connected their lands in western Carolina and eastern Tennessee.

The London Bald Trail is closest to the campground property. Reached from Piercy Creek, the London Bald Trail connects to Laurel Creek and Diamond Valley trails to provide numerous loop-hiking opportunities. Also, the Bartram National Scenic Trail is easily reached via the London Bald Trail. Consult the campground office for a hiking map.

Adjacent to the campground is a cool, clear fishing pond. An old-fashioned waterwheel oxygenates the water, where trout thrive. For stream fishing, head to nearby Piercy Creek. Nantahala Lake is just a few miles east for lake-fishing possibilities. An assortment of mountain biking trails threads the national forest-land nearby, which nearly envelops the campground.

Combine the fine, new facilities of Nelson's Nantahala Hideaway with the recreational variety of this section of western North Carolina and you have a successful tent-camping adventure.

MAP

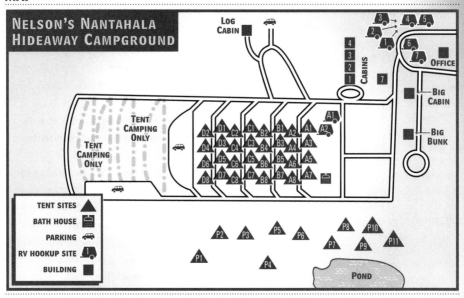

NELSON'S NANTAHALA HIDEAWAY CAMPGROUND

LOG CABIN

CABINS

OFFICE

BIG CABIN

BIG BUNK

TENT CAMPING ONLY

TENT CAMPING ONLY

D2 D1 C2 C1 B2 B1 A2 A1 A2 A1

D4 D3 C4 C3 B4 B3 A4 A3

D6 D5 C6 C5 B6 B5 A6 A5

D8 D7 C8 C7 B8 B7 A8 A7

TENT SITES

BATH HOUSE

PARKING

RV HOOKUP SITE

BUILDING

P1 P2 P3 P4 P5 P6 P7 P8 P9 P10 P11

POND

GETTING THERE

From Andrews take US 19/74 north for 6 miles to the community of Topton. Nelson's Nantahala Hideaway will be on your right.

NEW RIVER STATE PARK

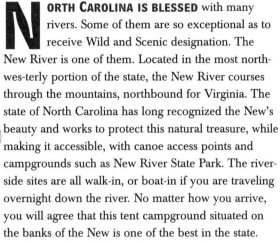

> *This tent campground on the banks of the New River is one of the best in the state.*

NORTH CAROLINA IS BLESSED with many rivers. Some of them are so exceptional as to receive Wild and Scenic designation. The New River is one of them. Located in the most north-wes-terly portion of the state, the New River courses through the mountains, northbound for Virginia. The state of North Carolina has long recognized the New's beauty and works to protect this natural treasure, while making it accessible, with canoe access points and campgrounds such as New River State Park. The river-side sites are all walk-in, or boat-in if you are traveling overnight down the river. No matter how you arrive, you will agree that this tent campground situated on the banks of the New is one of the best in the state.

Leave the walk-in parking area and cross a mown field, passing the remains of an old homestead with the chimney still standing. Reach campsite 9, sitting all alone in a small flat beside the spring run of the old homesite. Beyond here, the forest is regenerating in formerly plowed fields. A mix of black walnut, locust, and tulip trees shade the area amid thick brush. Mown paths reach the campsites. Campsite 8 is circled by brush and shaded by cherry trees. Cross a little wet-weather stream and enter the rest of the campground. Campsite 7 is directly along the river and is shaded by walnut trees. Campsite 6 is also along the river, but a steep bank prevents direct river access. The camp-ground operates its own river landing, and park per-sonnel encourage using only this access to keep down erosion. Campsite 5 is adjacent to campsite 6.

Campsite 4 is on a slight slope, but landscaping timbers have been added to level the camp beneath crab apple trees. Campsite 3 is closest to the bath-house, which is heated in the cooler months. Located beside the campground river access, campsite 2 is the park's most popular, especially with boat-in campers.

RATINGS

Beauty: ✿ ✿ ✿ ✿
Privacy: ✿ ✿ ✿ ✿
Spaciousness: ✿ ✿ ✿ ✿ ✿
Quiet: ✿ ✿ ✿ ✿ ✿
Security: ✿ ✿ ✿ ✿
Cleanliness: ✿ ✿ ✿ ✿

Tulip trees shade this site. Campsite 1 is also near the boat access, but is farther into the woods and is heavily shaded. This campground at the Wagoner Access fills on holiday weekends only. It can get a little busy at the beginning and end of summer. Sites are always available on weekdays. Critters such as raccoons abound in this area, so secure your food while camping here.

Most folks who camp here like to paddle the river. But even if you camp here as a non-boater, you can still have a good time. The mile-plus Fern Nature Trail circles the valley beside the campground. Add a mile and connect with the Running Cedar Trail. A pretty picnic area, once an apple orchard, lies adjacent to the camping area. The trees still produce fruit, attracting deer and humans alike in fall. A rapid drops just above the campground access, offering fishing opportunities and a decent little swimming hole below the rapid. A large field below the parking area allows room for games and general running around.

But face it, this park was developed with the paddler in mind. The state manages 26 miles of river here and maintains several access points for day and overnight trips. A popular run here is from the NC 88 bridge down to Wagoner Access, 5 miles in length. From Wagoner Access to the US 221 Access is 11 miles; plan for an all day trip. Paddling times vary with river flows and weather conditions. Also, trips run slower if you like to fish your way downriver as I do. Angling here is good for smallmouth bass, rock bass, and bream. Determined anglers might land a muskie.

An outfitter is located nearby if you are boatless or just want a shuttle. Contact Zaloo's Canoes. They offer inner tubes for fun, canoes for rent, or shuttle services of varying lengths. Reservations are required. For more information, call (800) 535-4027, or visit www.zaloos.com. The river scenery is both mountainous and pastoral, deserving of its wild and scenic status. Rapids are mild, not exceeding Class 2, making this a great training river. After you enjoy the Wagoner Access on the New, it will make you want to check out other state park access areas that lie along this preserved water in the state's northwest corner.

ADDRESS: New River State Park
P.O. Box 48
Jefferson, NC 28640

OPERATED BY: North Carolina State Parks

INFORMATION: (336) 982-2587; www.ncsparks.net

OPEN: Year-round

SITES: 9

EACH SITE HAS: Picnic table, fire grate, trash can

ASSIGNMENT: First come, first served; no reservation

REGISTRATION: Ranger will come by and register you

FACILITIES: Hot showers, flush toilets, water spigots

PARKING: At lot below ranger station

FEE: $8 per night

ELEVATION: 2,600 feet

RESTRICTIONS: **Pets:** On leash only
Fires: In fire rings only
Alcohol: Prohibited
Vehicles: None
Other: 14-day stay limit in a 30-day period

MAP

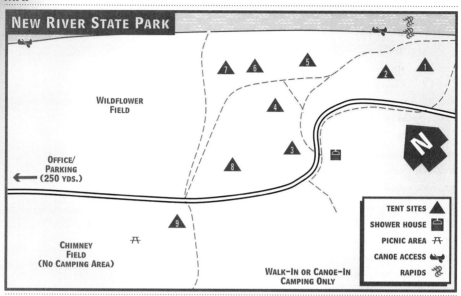

NEW RIVER STATE PARK

WILDFLOWER
FIELD

OFFICE/
PARKING
← (250 YDS.)

CHIMNEY
FIELD
(NO CAMPING AREA)

WALK-IN OR CANOE-IN
CAMPING ONLY

TENT SITES
SHOWER HOUSE
PICNIC AREA
CANOE ACCESS
RAPIDS

GETTING THERE

From the junction with US
421 on the west side of
Wilkesboro, take NC 16
north for 23 miles to NC 88.
Turn right, heading east on
NC 88 and follow it 1.4
miles to Wagoner Access
Road. Turn left on Wagoner
Access Road and follow it
one mile to enter the park.

NORTH MILLS RIVER CAMPGROUND

NORTH MILLS RIVER CAMPGROUND lies on the very edge of the Pisgah National Forest. The sylvan setting of the campground is divided by the free-flowing North Mills River, which has cut a valley amid the Carolina mountains. All roads leading to and within the campground are paved, which lures in a few extra RVers. Overall, this is an unhurried, family-atmosphere campground that is rarely filled to capacity.

As you approach the campground, it seems much larger than it really is, due to the sizable picnic area adjacent to the campground. To your right is a half-moon-shaped camping loop containing 13 campsites. These sites are in a very level area lying between the North Mills River and a steep hill. Tall shade trees grow high over the grassy understory. The five sites inside the half-moon are spread far apart and are very open. These sites are for the campers with excess gear who don't mind a slight sacrifice in privacy. Some sites on the outskirts of the loop, where the campground host resides, are set into the hillside and are less level. Four water spigots are evenly spaced among the campsites. A comfort station with flush toilets is at the loop's center.

Over a bridge across the North Mills River is the main campground loop. These 19 sites are on a slight slope declining toward the river. As you drive along the one-way road, look for a field inside the loop that contains four spacious and open sites. One of these is a double site for groups. A short spur road dead-ends off this loop and leads to three smaller campsites; this trio offers the most isolation in the entire campground.

As you continue along the main loop, the field gives way to an understory of hemlock, fern, and rhododendron growing among nearly hidden campsites. This understory grows very thick, especially as

> *North Mills River Campground offers a worthy sampling of the southern Blue Ridge country.*

RATINGS

Beauty: ✿ ✿ ✿
Privacy: ✿ ✿ ✿ ✿
Spaciousness: ✿ ✿ ✿ ✿
Quiet: ✿ ✿ ✿ ✿
Security: ✿ ✿ ✿ ✿
Cleanliness: ✿ ✿ ✿ ✿

ADDRESS:	North Mills River Campground P.O. Box 8 Pisgah Forest, NC 28768
OPERATED BY:	U.S. Forest Service
INFORMATION:	(828) 877-3265; www.cs.unca.edu/nfs nc
OPEN:	Entire campground, mid-March–October; some sites, year-round
SITES:	31
EACH SITE HAS:	Tent pad, fire grate, lantern post, picnic table
ASSIGNMENT:	By reservation or first come, first served
REGISTRATION:	Self-registration on site; reserve by phone (877) 444-6777, or online at www.reserveusa.com
FACILITIES:	Water and flush toilets in spring, summer, and fall; no water and only chemical toilets in winter
PARKING:	At campsites only
FEE:	$8 per night, $11 per night for premium sites along the river
ELEVATION:	2,500 feet
RESTRICTIONS:	Pets: On leash only Fires: In fire grates only Alcohol: At campsites only Vehicles: None Other: 14-day stay limit

the loop parallels the river. Three single sites and one double site are located riverside beneath tall evergreens. Four water spigots are situated along the loop. A lighted bathroom lies in the dark and forested center of the loop.

North Mills River is used mostly by local families. Children float down the river in inner tubes, and anglers fish for trout, while others explore the nearby forest trails. As summer evenings darken and cool down, campers often meander from site to site and get to know their neighbors. Don't be surprised if you are paid a friendly visit and offered a cup of coffee by your fellow camper. The campground host is often the center of these social gatherings.

To get a good lay of the land combined with a little history, take a scenic forest drive. Gravel Forest Service Road 1206 leaves the campground just beyond the self-service pay station. It will lead you to the Pink Beds Visitor Center. The Pink Beds is a 6,800-acre mountain valley where professional forestry was first practiced in the United States. It is a National Historic Site complete with a museum that tells of the evolution of forestry in our country. Two interpretive trails enhance the story of George Vanderbilt's management of his forestland. This valley is also known as the Cradle of Forestry in America.

To complete your scenic drive, turn right on US 276 from the Pink Beds and intersect the Blue Ridge Parkway after 3.8 miles. The Blue Ridge Parkway extends 469 miles, to link the Great Smoky Mountains and Shenandoah national parks. Head north on the parkway and enjoy some of the scenery for which this road is known. Stop and climb the 1-mile Frying Pan Mountain Trail to the lookout tower at its peak. Farther north is your right turn back onto gravel Forest Service 479 and back down to the Mills River Recreation Area.

Informal hiking and fishing trails fan out from the campground. Several marked trails start 2 miles from the campground up FS 479 just after its junction with FS 142. The Big Creek Trail (102) and Trace Ridge Trail (354) are two trails of note. They both leave the North Mills River watershed to intersect the Blue

MAP

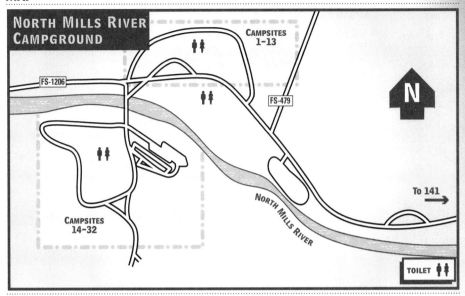

NORTH MILLS RIVER CAMPGROUND

CAMPSITES 1-13

FS-1206

FS-479

N

To 141

NORTH MILLS RIVER

CAMPSITES 14-32

TOILET

Ridge Parkway and the high country. If you're not sure exactly where to go, just ask your neighbor. Most local folks in the campground will gladly steer you onto a nearby good path. After all, they're quite proud of their mountain lands.

GETTING THERE

From Asheville follow NC 191 south for 13.3 miles to North Mills River Road (NC 1345). Turn right at the campground sign and follow North Mills River Road for 5 miles, intersecting the North Mills River Campground.

PRICE PARK
CAMPGROUND

> *This campground is part of the Blue Ridge Parkway, yet it offers more than just a stopping place between scenic drives.*

LOCATED HIGH IN THE FORESTS of the Blue Ridge Mountains, Price Park has a quality campground and plenty of activities that don't involve an automobile. Don't let the size of the campground scare you off. There are nearly 200 sites in three areas; one area for RV-camping only, one for one-night campers only, and another for both RV and tent camping.

The one-night-only camping loop is backed against the shores of Price Lake. The south end of the paved loop is thickly forested, both overhead and on the ground for maximum privacy. Five of the sites are right along the lakeshore. The other end of the loop circles a field and is more open. A few pull-through RV sites are here. A lighted bathroom is conveniently placed at the center of the loop for all campers to share. Two water spigots are located at each end of this spacious and private loop.

The main RV/tent area has three loops. Loops C and D spur off the larger Loop B. Oddly enough, Loop D is actually inside Loop B. Loop C spurs off on its own. They are all in a rolling woodland and tastefully set into the mountains without dominating the natural landscape. The plethora of trees overhead reminds you that you are in the forest. The rhododendron understory provides enough privacy; however, it isn't everywhere, which allows you to move about the campground freely.

Landscaping timbers were used where site leveling was necessary. Some of the sites in Loops B and C are a tad close together, but with investigating and luck, you can find a private site. Nine water spigots are scattered throughout these three loops for easy water access. Three lighted bathrooms ensure you never have to go too far if nature calls in the middle of the night.

RATINGS

Beauty: ✿ ✿ ✿ ✿ ✿
Privacy: ✿ ✿ ✿
Spaciousness: ✿ ✿ ✿ ✿
Quiet: ✿ ✿ ✿ ✿
Security: ✿ ✿ ✿ ✿
Cleanliness: ✿ ✿ ✿ ✿ ✿

Loops E and F are for RVs only and concentrate these campers in one location. On my visit to Price Park, I didn't see any other RVers outside the RV-only loops, with the exception of a couple in the one-night-only loop. Expect a full house on hot summer weekends when nearby lowlanders escape the heat. A ranger and a campground host reside at the campground to answer questions and ease your safety concerns.

Even the most ardent auto tourists have to stretch their legs every once in a while and see for themselves just what is beyond the roadside. Price Park offers the Blue Ridge sightseer plenty to do outside the car. Trails actually run through the campground, which makes starting a hike even easier.

The Boone Fork Trail makes a 5-mile loop passing through many environments of the Blue Ridge. It leaves the campground to enter a meadow and picks up an old farm road. It then runs along Bee Tree Creek, crossing it 16 times. Pass through a rocky area and return to the campground through a meadow.

The 2.3-mile Green Knob Trail climbs to an overlook that will reward you with well-earned views of Price Lake, then loops back via Sims Pond. The Tanawha Trail runs for 13 miles south along the Blue Ridge Parkway and obviously requires a shuttle. A segment of the nearly complete North Carolina Mountains-to-Sea Trail passes through Price Park on its way to the Atlantic.

The Price Lake Trail makes a 2.3-mile loop around the 47-acre Price Lake. The lake contains three species of trout that you can angle for: rainbow, brook, and brown. Nearby Sims Pond has only the native brook trout. Stream fishermen can try Boone Fork and Sims Creek for trout as well. A valid North Carolina fishing license is required.

During the 1940s, Julian Price bought this area as a retreat for his company employees. His heirs willed the area to the park service for all of us to enjoy. As scenic as the Blue Ridge Parkway is, you may find this special area hard to pass by. Stop and spend a day enjoying the Blue Ridge with no glass between you and nature.

KEY INFORMATION

ADDRESS: Price Park Campground 199 Hamphill Knob Road Asheville, NC 28801

OPERATED BY: National Park Service

INFORMATION: (828) 298-0398; www.nps.gov/blri

OPEN: May 1–October 31

SITES: 129

EACH SITE HAS: Tent pad, picnic table, fire grate, lantern post

ASSIGNMENT: First come, first served; no reservations

REGISTRATION: Register at campground check-in station

FACILITIES: Water, flush toilets, pay phone, concessions served on main road in spring and summer

PARKING: At campsites only

FEE: $12 per night for 2 people; $2 each additional person over 18

ELEVATION: 3,400 feet

RESTRICTIONS: Pets: On 6-foot or shorter leash
Fires: In fire grates only
Alcohol: At campsites only
Vehicles: 30-foot trailer length limit
Other: 14-day stay limit, 30-day total limit for calendar year

MAP

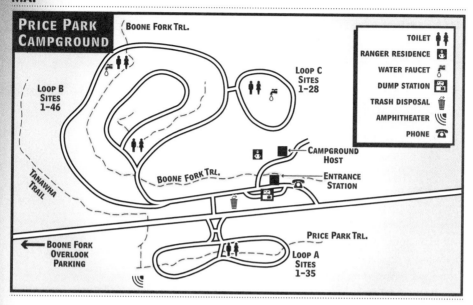

PRICE PARK CAMPGROUND

BOONE FORK TRL.

LOOP B SITES 1-46

LOOP C SITES 1-28

TANAWHA TRAIL

BOONE FORK TRL.

CAMPGROUND HOST

ENTRANCE STATION

BOONE FORK OVERLOOK PARKING

PRICE PARK TRL.

LOOP A SITES 1-35

TOILET	👥
RANGER RESIDENCE	🏠
WATER FAUCET	🚰
DUMP STATION	🚉
TRASH DISPOSAL	🗑
AMPHITHEATER	📢
PHONE	☎

GETTING THERE

From Boone take US 321 east for 7 miles to the Blue Ridge Parkway. Turn south on the parkway and follow it for 7 miles to Julian Price Memorial Park. The campground check-in station will be on your right.

ROCKY BLUFF
CAMPGROUND

> *The design of this campground will capture your fancy and the setting will make you stay.*

AS I HEADED DOWN into the Rocky Bluff Recreation Area, I found it hard to believe there was a campground down there. The road dipped into very hilly terrain, with nary a flat spot to be found. But soon enough there was the beginning of Rocky Bluff Campground. "Engineering marvel" may be a stretch, but a ton or two of site leveling and stonework had to be done to tastefully fit this campground into the wooded dips and rises of the land. All the stonework makes your back ache just looking at it.

Rocky Bluff Campground is divided into two loops. Enter the lower loop as you pass the pay station. Three shaded sites are dug into the hillside and reinforced with the above-mentioned stonework. Five open sites sit on the inside of the loop and are on what passes for flat ground here at Rocky Bluff.

At the low point of the lower loop, a road spurs off to the right and leads to the upper loop. As the road makes a steep climb, two campsites are somehow fit into the terrain. Seven sites lie on top of the hill, spread along the road as it makes a short loop to return to the main campground. Two sites feature a view into Spring Creek hollow to the east.

A warning to those who get spooked easily: Also atop this hill, right next to the campsites, is the Brooks Cemetery. Three sites have a view of the cemetery. Stay down on the lower loop if the proximity of the cemetery will prevent you from enjoying a sound night's sleep.

Intersect the lower loop again from the upper loop road. There, sites are strewn in the open, lightly wooded center of the loop; a few more are tucked away in the thickets outside the loop. There isn't a whole lot of privacy. Due to the sloping terrain, you are probably going to be looking down on another camper or vice versa. And a generally grassy under-

RATINGS

Beauty: ✪ ✪ ✪ ✪ ✪
Privacy: ✪ ✪ ✪
Spaciousness: ✪ ✪ ✪
Quiet: ✪ ✪ ✪ ✪
Security: ✪ ✪ ✪ ✪
Cleanliness: ✪ ✪ ✪ ✪

ADDRESS:	Rocky Bluff Campground P.O. Box 128 Hot Springs, NC 28743
OPERATED BY:	U.S. Forest Service
INFORMATION:	(828) 622-3202; www.cs.unca.edu/nfsnc
OPEN:	May 1–October 31
SITES:	30
EACH SITE HAS:	Tent pad, fire grate, lantern post, picnic table
ASSIGNMENT:	First come, first served; no reservations
REGISTRATION:	Self-registration on site
FACILITIES:	Water, flush toilets
PARKING:	At campsites only
FEE:	$8 per night
ELEVATION:	1,780 feet
RESTRICTIONS:	**Pets:** On 6-foot or shorter leash **Fires:** In fire grates only **Alcohol:** At campsites only **Vehicles:** 18-foot trailer length limit **Other:** 14-day stay limit

story doesn't shield you much from your neighbor, either. The upper loop is more wooded, where ironically you might want to keep your neighbor in view to make sure he isn't a ghost roaming from the cemetery.

The lower loop road passes a picnic area on the right and returns to the pay station. This loop has the only comfort station for the 30-site campground. Those on the upper loop must walk down the hill to use the facilities. But water spigots are conveniently placed around both loops for your convenience.

This campground is neat. The terrain and stonework make it unique. The cemetery adds a touch of history and mystique. If the cemetery isn't enough of the past, imagine this place a century ago when there was a community of homes, a blacksmith shop, and even a school!

The nearest community, Hot Springs, embodies small town Appalachia—full of nice people who work hard for a living in the splendor of a land that is now more precious to them than ever before. The Appalachian Trail runs right through town. Visit the Pisgah National Forest Visitor Center. And you've got to check out the hot springs for which the community was named.

Outdoor pastimes are plentiful. Several outfitters in town will arrange a whitewater rafting trip down the French Broad, which flows through Hot Springs. A 6-mile biking trail runs along the river to Paint Rock, which marks the Tennessee–North Carolina state line. This dividing line crosses the bridge over the French Broad from Hot Springs. The AT crosses this bridge too. Hike either way on the AT until your legs wear out.

Two fulfilling trails depart from Rocky Bluff Campground. The 1.2-mile Spring Creek Nature Trail loops down to Spring Creek and follows it a good way before veering north and intersecting the campground again. This is a rewarding and short day hike. The Van Cliff Loop Trail is a little longer and tougher. It leaves the campground and climbs, crossing NC 209 on the way. The trail hooks up into some piney woods before returning to the welcome campground after 2.6 miles.

MAP

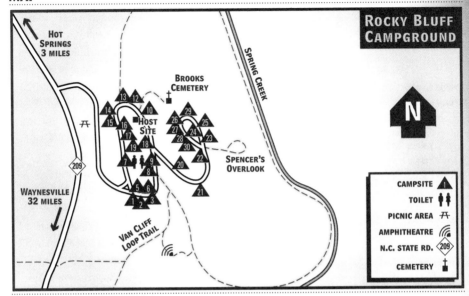

ROCKY BLUFF CAMPGROUND

HOT SPRINGS 3 MILES

SPRING CREEK

BROOKS CEMETERY

HOST SITE

13 12
14 10
15 16
17
19 18
7 9
8
5 6
1 2 3
4

26 29
27 25
28 24 23
30
20 22
21

SPENCER'S OVERLOOK

WAYNESVILLE 32 MILES

VAN CLIFF LOOP TRAIL

N

CAMPSITE ▲ 1
TOILET 👤👤
PICNIC AREA ⊓
AMPHITHEATRE 🔊
N.C. STATE RD. ⟨209⟩
CEMETERY †

GETTING THERE

From Hot Springs take NC 209 south for 3 miles. Rocky Bluff Campground will be on your left.

STANDING INDIAN
CAMPGROUND

> *Soak in the mountains of the Standing Indian Basin from the headwaters of the Nantahala River.*

ACCORDING TO **C**HEROKEE LEGEND, a warrior was once posted on top of a certain mountain to look out for a flying monster that had swept away a child from a nearby village. The villagers prayed to the Great Spirit to annihilate the monster. A violent storm struck the mountain reducing it to rock, turning the lookout warrior into a stone "Standing Indian."

The Nantahala River is born on Standing Indian Mountain just upstream from this outstanding, high-country campground, where cool breezes from the ridge tops temper the warm summer air. With sites on five loops, the campground is spread out and offers the camper varying site conditions. The first loop diffuses along the Nantahala with hemlock-shaded sites isolated by thick stands of rhododendron. Across the river, three loops are spread out in a large, flat area interspersed with large hardwoods that allow plenty of sun and grass to flourish among their ranks. Ritter Lumber Company once had a logging camp here. Farther back still, across Kimsey Creek, are mountainside sites. They stand level, among the sloping forest of yellow birch, beech, and sugar maple, separated by lush greenery that makes each site seem isolated. Six double sites accommodate larger groups.

Campground hosts occupy each loop for your safety and convenience. Sixteen water pumps are strategically located throughout the loops, in addition to five comfort stations with flush toilets. Two of the comfort stations have hot showers. There are no electric hookups. You may pick up dead, downed firewood from the surrounding area without a permit. Keep in mind that Standing Indian can be crowded during peak summer weekends.

There's plenty to do nearby. Try your luck at one of the campground horseshoe pits. Fish for trout on the Nantahala River or Kimsey Creek. Rainbow and

RATINGS

Beauty: ✿ ✿ ✿ ✿ ✿
Privacy: ✿ ✿ ✿ ✿
Spaciousness: ✿ ✿ ✿ ✿ ✿
Quiet: ✿ ✿ ✿
Security: ✿ ✿ ✿ ✿
Cleanliness: ✿ ✿ ✿ ✿

brown trout are the predominant cold-water fish in the streams, with some brook trout in the upper waters. For the nonfishing water lover, there are two falls nearby. Drive 5 miles on Forest Service Road 67 beyond the turnoff to the campground. The Big Laurel Falls Trail sign is on the right. After passing over a footbridge, the trail splits. Veer to the right and come to Big Laurel Falls in 0.5 miles. The Mooney Falls Trail starts 0.7 miles beyond the Big Laurel Falls trailhead and leads 0.1 mile to the cascading falls.

Several trails begin at the campground itself. To orient yourself, find the Backcountry Information Center located 0.2 miles left of the campground entrance gate. Study the map. Make an 8-mile loop out of the Park Creek and Park Ridge trails. The Park Creek Trail starts at the Backcountry Information Center. Follow it down the Nantahala then up Park Creek to Park Gap. Take the Park Ridge Trail 3.2 miles back down to the campground. This hike is rated moderate to strenuous, with a net elevation change of 880 feet.

The most prominent trail in the area is the famed Appalachian Trail, which skirts the campground to the south and east. This 87-mile section from the Georgia line to the Smokies is considered by many hikers to be one of the most rugged sections, with its relentlessly steep ups and downs. This section weeds out many AT thru-hikers who aspire to "follow the white blaze" 2,100 miles to Maine.

The AT passes by FS 67 on the way to the campground. Drive out of the campground toward Wallace Gap about a mile. The Rock Gap parking area is on your right. Take the AT south (uphill to your right) and soon you'll come to the Rock Gap backcountry shelter. These shelters are located about one day's walk from one another along the entire AT. They provide a haven from the elements for the weary thru-hiker. Imagine this as your home for a six-month journey up the spine of the Appalachians.

While you're at Standing Indian Campground, why not see the mountain it was named for? It's a strenuous 3.9-mile climb to the 5,499-foot peak, but the views provide ample reward. Use the Lower Ridge Trail, which starts on the left just beyond the camp-

MAP

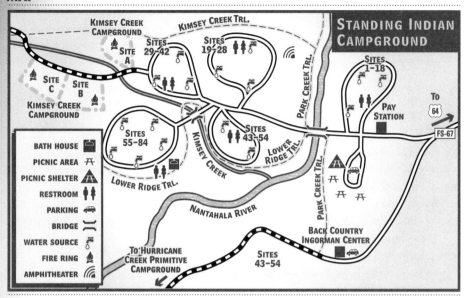

STANDING INDIAN CAMPGROUND

KIMSEY CREEK CAMPGROUND

KIMSEY CREEK TRL.

SITE A
SITES 29-42
SITES 19-28
PARK CREEK TRL.
SITES 1-18
PAY STATION
To 64
FS-67

SITE C
SITE B
KIMSEY CREEK CAMPGROUND

SITES 55-84
KIMSEY CREEK
SITES 43-54
LOWER RIDGE TRL.
PARK CREEK TRL.

LOWER RIDGE TRL.

NANTAHALA RIVER

BACK COUNTRY INGORMAN CENTER

To HURRICANE CREEK PRIMITIVE CAMPGROUND
SITES 43-54

Legend

- BATH HOUSE
- PICNIC AREA
- PICNIC SHELTER
- RESTROOM
- PARKING
- BRIDGE
- WATER SOURCE
- FIRE RING
- AMPHITHEATER

GETTING THERE

From Franklin drive west on US 64 for 9 miles to old US 64. Following the sign to Standing Indian, turn left and go 1.5 miles to Wallace Gap. Turn right at the sign on FS 67 leading to the campground.

ground bridge over the Nantahala. Switchback up to the ridgecrest and follow it southward to the AT. Take a spur trail 0.2 miles to the top of Standing Indian. View the Blue Ridge Mountains and the Tallulah River Basin.

STONE MOUNTAIN STATE PARK

Elkin

PERCHED ON THE EASTERN EDGE of the Blue Ridge Mountains, Stone Mountain State Park is a 13,000-acre preserve of granite domes and hardwoods, where wild trout streams and hiking trails thread the land. Stone Mountain Campground, quiet and punctuated with just the right amenities, merely clinches the decision to visit here.

Stone Mountain Campground is situated in a mixed hardwood forest adjacent to a grassy meadow. Two loops provide Stone Mountain tent campers, who compose 90% of the campground users, with a variety of campsite settings.

The first campground loop lies in the shade of moderately sloping woodland. The 13 sites are carved out of a second-growth forest that provides optimum privacy due to the thick stands of young, straight trees racing skyward to the light. The dense growth limits campsite spaciousness, yet offers adequate room for all but the biggest gearheads.

Five of the sites are on the loop's interior, making them closest to the modern comfort station. It includes hot showers, flush toilets for each sex, drinking water, and laundry tubs for those dirty clothes. Piped water is just a few steps away no matter where you are on this loop.

Six more sites abut the open field along the main campground road. Bushes are planted here and there for a little privacy, but these sites are still very open. Maximum site spaciousness offsets the lack of privacy. Tent campers who like plenty of sunshine will enjoy these sites.

Farther along the road is a mix of forest and field. The campground host cabin sits here amid wooded sites on one side of the paved road. The other side of the road features a continuation of the open sites. The road makes a small loop, containing five campsites that

> *The 13,000-acre Stone Mountain State Park is a designated National Natural Landmark.*

RATINGS

Beauty: ✿ ✿ ✿
Privacy: ✿ ✿ ✿ ✿
Spaciousness: ✿ ✿ ✿ ✿
Quiet: ✿ ✿ ✿ ✿
Security: ✿ ✿ ✿ ✿ ✿
Cleanliness: ✿ ✿ ✿ ✿ ✿

ADDRESS: Stone Mountain
State Park
3600 Frank Parkway
Roaring Gap, NC
28668

OPERATED BY: North Carolina State
Parks

INFORMATION: (336) 957-8185;
ils.unc.edu/park
project/ncparks.html

OPEN: Year-round

SITES: 37

EACH SITE HAS: Tent pad, fire grate,
grill, picnic table

ASSIGNMENT: First come, first
served; no reserva-
tions

REGISTRATION: Campground host
will come around
and register campers

FACILITIES: Water, flush toilets,
hot showers, pay
phone

PARKING: At campsites only

FEE: $12 per night

ELEVATION: 2,000 feet

RESTRICTIONS: **Pets:** On 6-foot or
shorter leash
Fires: In fire grates
only
Alcohol: Not allowed
Vehicles: None
Other: 14-day stay
limit

are the most private in the entire campground. There is piped water nearby, but you must walk to the first loop to access the campground's only comfort station.

A campground host and active, friendly rangers make this a safe and fun place. Park gates open at 8 a.m. and close at sunset. With all that is going on here at Stone Mountain, this campground fills up on summer weekends. Rangers lead interpretive programs teaching about this area's natural and cultural riches.

The granite dome of Stone Mountain is the centerpiece of this park. View the dome from the park office. Rock climbers can be seen scaling the sheer face. If you should engage in this challenging endeavor, register at the park office (and the local hospital, too). A marked hiking trail will lead you to the top of the dome safely.

The trails around Stone Mountain, with the exception of Widows Creek Trail, are interconnected, making a variety of loops possible. Start at the main trail parking area at the base of Stone Mountain. It is a short but steep 0.6 miles to the summit of the dome on the Stone Mountain Trail. Westward is the crest of the Blue Ridge. If you continue on, you'll encounter Hitching Rock. There, other prominent park features, Wolf Rock and Cedar Rock, can be seen. Next, pass the 200-foot Stone Mountain Falls on Big Sandy Creek. Complete your loop at 3.3 miles.

Cedar Rock and Wolf Rock trails are rewarding hikes and allow good views of Stone Mountain. The self-guided Nature Trail will familiarize you with the flora of the area. The Widows Creek Trail leads into the isolated northwestern section of the park, where backcountry campers stay overnight.

Trout fishing is a popular pursuit here. Rainbow, brown, and brook trout are all represented in the 17 miles of mountain streams. These waters are accessible along roads and foot trails. Check with the park office, as the creeks have varying fishing regulations.

Stone Mountain has been in the works for millions of years, yet we have only made our mark relatively recently. After all the time devoted to its development, Stone Mountain is worth more than a few days of your time.

MAP

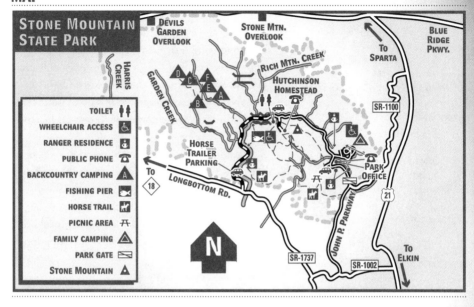

STONE MOUNTAIN STATE PARK

DEVILS GARDEN OVERLOOK

STONE MTN. OVERLOOK

BLUE RIDGE PKWY.

To SPARTA

HARRIS CREEK

GARDEN CREEK

RICH MTN. CREEK

HUTCHINSON HOMESTEAD

SR-1100

Legend	
TOILET	👫
WHEELCHAIR ACCESS	♿
RANGER RESIDENCE	🏠
PUBLIC PHONE	☎
BACKCOUNTRY CAMPING	⛺
FISHING PIER	🎣
HORSE TRAIL	🐎
PICNIC AREA	⛱
FAMILY CAMPING	⛺
PARK GATE	✉
STONE MOUNTAIN	⛰

HORSE TRAILER PARKING

To 18 LONGBOTTOM RD.

PARK OFFICE

JOHN P. PARKWAY

21

To ELKIN

SR-1737

SR-1002

N

GETTING THERE

From Elkin drive north on US 21 for 13 miles to Traphill Road (SR 1002). There will be a sign for the park. Turn left on Traphill Road, following it for 4.3 miles to John P. Frank Parkway. Turn right at the parkway and follow it for 2.5 miles to the park entrance.

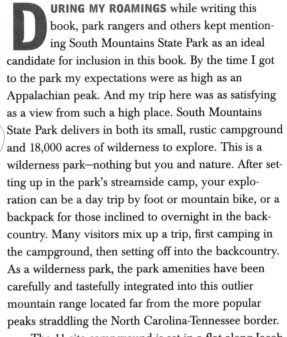

Morganton

SOUTH MOUNTAINS
STATE PARK

> *Tent campers will love this rugged backwoods state park with an emphasis on wilderness.*

DURING MY ROAMINGS while writing this book, park rangers and others kept mentioning South Mountains State Park as an ideal candidate for inclusion in this book. By the time I got to the park my expectations were as high as an Appalachian peak. And my trip here was as satisfying as a view from such a high place. South Mountains State Park delivers in both its small, rustic campground and 18,000 acres of wilderness to explore. This is a wilderness park—nothing but you and nature. After setting up in the park's streamside camp, your exploration can be a day trip by foot or mountain bike, or a backpack for those inclined to overnight in the backcountry. Many visitors mix up a trip, first camping in the campground, then setting off into the backcountry. As a wilderness park, the park amenities have been carefully and tastefully integrated into this outlier mountain range located far from the more popular peaks straddling the North Carolina-Tennessee border.

The 11-site campground is set in a flat along Jacob Fork, a crystalline, musical trout stream tumbling over gray rocks that resonates among the campsites. Immediately reach campsite 1. Landscaping timbers delineate each site and corral small gravel within the tent pads for campsite drainage. Each site's "fittings," i.e. picnic table and lantern post, are in fine condition. Tall, straight tulip trees and white pines shade the campground, along with hemlock, sourwood, hickory, maple, and sweetgum. Campsite 2 is across the campground road from Jacob Fork. Campsite 3 and 4 are near the creek and are backed up against mountain laurel and rhododendron. More sites are set directly along the creek. Campsite 7 is a handicap site and has a wide picnic table. Campsite 8 has many hemlocks overhead. I wish I had stayed in campsite 9, which backs directly against the stream and overlooks a steep

RATINGS

Beauty: ✿ ✿ ✿ ✿ ✿
Privacy: ✿ ✿ ✿
Spaciousness: ✿ ✿ ✿
Quiet: ✿ ✿ ✿ ✿
Security: ✿ ✿ ✿ ✿ ✿
Cleanliness: ✿ ✿ ✿ ✿

hillside. Campsite 10 is also beside Jacob Fork. Unfortunately, I arrived just at dark and didn't want to bother other campers by driving through the campground multiple times, even though I normally "loop the loop" before choosing a site. Campsite 11, the last in the lineup, was my choice. The modern vault toilet and water spigot were conveniently close to this campsite.

I enjoyed being deep in this mountain valley. So do others, as the small campground will fill most summer weekends. I recommend fall or spring, when the campground is wide open. During spring the wildflowers will be blooming and the creeks running high, which makes the many waterfalls and cascades more enticing. In fall, the colors will be every bit as good as the main Appalachian Range, but less busy. Campers can get a site any time of year during the week.

The South Mountains range from 1,200 to around 3,000 feet high. That makes visiting them more appealing in spring and fall, as they will be less chilly than other, higher ranges. Summer can be warm but is not oppressively hot. The park has 40 miles of trails to explore, ranging from a 0.75-mile interpretive nature trail along Jacob Fork, very worth your time, to loops long enough for you to bring your sleeping bag should you attempt them. More popular day hikes are to High Shoals Falls, which can be made into a loop hike, to Little River Falls, and to Jacob Knob Overlook. A quality park trail map reveals other loop possibilities. The many park streams offer trout fishing in an attractive setting. Not only does the park contain the entire Jacob Fork watershed, but it has also acquired the Clear Creek and Henry Fork drainages. Anglers are limited only by time and desire. Be apprised of the latest license requirements and fishing regulations before you strike out.

Mountain bikers have an 18-mile designated loop that the park deems strenuous, so be prepared for an all day outing on this path that circles the ridge lines along Jacob Creek—and bring your water bottle. After my experience at South Mountains State Park, I will be circling back to this place for more of the best in tent camping.

KEY INFORMATION

ADDRESS: South Mountains State Park 3001 South Mountains State Park Avenue Connelly Springs, NC 28612

OPERATED BY: North Carolina State Parks

INFORMATION: (828) 433-4772; www.ncsparks.net

OPEN: Year-round

SITES: 11

EACH SITE HAS: Picnic table, fire ring, lantern post, tent pad

ASSIGNMENT: First come, first served; no reservations

REGISTRATION: Ranger will come by and register you

FACILITIES: Vault toilets, water spigots

PARKING: At campsites only

FEE: $8 per night

ELEVATION: 1,350 feet

RESTRICTIONS: Pets: On leash only Fires: In fire rings only Alcohol: Prohibited Vehicles: 25-foot trailers or less recommended Other: 14-day stay limit

MAP

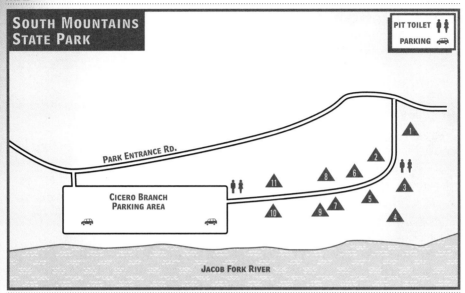

SOUTH MOUNTAINS
STATE PARK

PIT TOILET
PARKING

PARK ENTRANCE RD.

CICERO BRANCH
PARKING AREA

1
2
3
4
5
6
7
8
9
10
11

JACOB FORK RIVER

GETTING THERE

From exit 105 on I-40 near Morganton, take NC 18 south for 11 miles to Sugar Loaf Road. Turn right on Sugar Loaf Road and follow it for 2 miles, then turn left on Old 18 Road. Take Old 18 Road for 2.6 miles, then turn right on NC 1901, Wards Gap Road, follow it for 1.3 miles, and then veer right on South Mountain Park Road. Follow South Mountain Park Road for 3.5 miles to reach the campground.

SUNBURST CAMPGROUND

SUNBURST HAS AN INTERESTING NAME. It sounds like a high-dollar mountain resort, but the name originally belonged to a logging town. Today, visitors see nothing but a small, appealing campground that lies at the base of two wilderness areas, Shining Rock and Middle Prong. If you explore the trails of the wildernesses, you may run into old iron implements of the logging era, especially in the Middle Prong, along with a rich forest replete with wildflowers and clear mountain streams home to native brook trout. Shining Rock offers open high country meadows with far reaching views. I have hiked both wildernesses and heartily endorse their beauty. So pack your tent, hiking boots, and camera, then come on up to Sunburst.

Sunburst is the kind of campground that grows on you. At first sight, it seems a little small and a little too open, but the beauty of the overall area is readily apparent. After all, you drive a Forest Heritage Scenic Byway to get here. The 14 campsites are strung along a half-loop across a meadow from the West Fork Pigeon River. The steep reaches of Beartrail Ridge form the campground's backdrop. The large meadow between the river and the camping area avails views of the tall ridges towering over Sunburst.

The campsites, which lie between the gravel road and Beartrail Ridge, are adequately spaced from one another. The forest service has landscaped between the campsites with spruce, rhododendron, and hardwoods for added privacy. A campground host is stationed in the center of the sites, adding safety, information, and security to Sunburst. The camp bathroom is up the hill behind the host, and a small turnaround is situated at the far end of the camp, along with a picnic area for day visitors.

> *Sunburst is nestled at the base of two of North Carolina's best wilderness areas.*

RATINGS

Beauty: ✿ ✿ ✿
Privacy: ✿ ✿ ✿
Spaciousness: ✿ ✿ ✿
Quiet: ✿ ✿ ✿ ✿
Security: ✿ ✿ ✿ ✿
Cleanliness: ✿ ✿ ✿ ✿

KEY INFORMATION

ADDRESS: Sunburst
Campground
P.O. Box 8
Pisgah forest, NC
28768

OPERATED BY: Cradle of Forestry
Interpretive
Association

INFORMATION: (828) 877-3350;
www.cs.unca.edu/nfs
nc

OPEN: April–October

SITES: 14

EACH SITE HAS: Picnic table, fire
grate

ASSIGNMENT: First come, first
served; no reserva-
tions

REGISTRATION: Self-registration on
site

FACILITIES: Water spigot, vault
toilets

PARKING: At campsites only

FEE: $7 per night

ELEVATION: 3,100 feet

RESTRICTIONS: Pets: On leash only
Fires: In fire rings
only
Alcohol:
At campsites only
Vehicles: None
Other: 14-day stay
limit

I have enjoyed Sunburst in three seasons and it has never disappointed. Spring is the time of rebirth and, when on a fishing trip up nearby Middle Prong, I could hardly concentrate on my line, distracted by the wildflowers galore. Summertime found me up on the meadows and clearings of Shining Rock, which looms over the high country of the Black Mountains. The mountains were named for the dark mantle of spruce and fir that cloaks their highest points (I have also visited these peaks during winter—cold and snowy!). My latest trip took place on a warm fall day, when I toured the area by auto, watching strong winds return leaves from the hardwoods back to the earth.

A rewarding 11-mile hike in the Middle Prong Wilderness leaves Sunburst campground and follows nearby Forest Road 97 up to the Haywood Gap Trail. Head up Middle Prong, then on up Haywood Stream to Haywood Gap and the Blue Ridge Parkway. Then take the Mountains-to-Sea Trail along the crest of Pisgah Ridge down to the Buckeye Gap Trail, returning to Middle Prong. The fishing is good on Middle Prong as well as the West Fork Pigeon River. West Prong also has some big water holes that invite sweaty hikers to take a dip.

The easiest way to access Shining Rock Wilderness from Sunburst is to take NC 215 up to the Blue Ridge Parkway, then head north just a short distance. Or you could take the Fork Mountain Trail for a 6-mile hike that climbs nearly 3,000 feet. I'd drive if I were you, then park below Black Balsam Knob, 6,214 feet in elevation. From here, take the Art Loeb Trail over Black Balsam Knob and Tennent Mountain. Continue past Ivestor Gap and on to Shining Rock, where views await hikers atop white quartz outcrops. Return via the Ivestor Gap Trail for a loop of around 9 miles. Also nearby is Yellowstone Falls, off the Gravestone Fields Trail, and attractive falls along Laurel Creek on the Laurel Creek Trail. A map of the wildernesses is well worth the money and will keep you plenty busy on your trip to Sunburst.

MAP

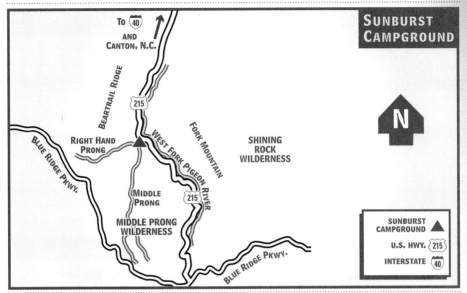

GETTING THERE

From exit 31 on I-40 near Canton, take North Carolina 215 south for 18 miles to Sunburst Campground, which will be on your right.

TSALI CAMPGROUND

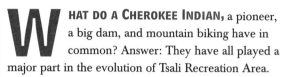

> *Head straight from the tent and go mountain biking, boating, horseback riding, hiking, or fishing.*

WHAT DO A **CHEROKEE INDIAN,** a pioneer, a big dam, and mountain biking have in common? Answer: They have all played a major part in the evolution of Tsali Recreation Area.

In 1838, during a forced removal of native peoples to the American West, which became known as the Trail of Tears, a Cherokee leader by the name of Tsali turned himself in so other Cherokee could remain in the area. These natives formed the nucleus of the Eastern Band of Cherokee who now live on the reservation adjacent to Bryson City. Early in this century, pioneer Harv Brown raised corn along Mouse Branch; there he turned his corn into "corn juice," otherwise known as moonshine. In the 1940s, when Fontana Dam was built, Harv and his kinfolk moved away. Now Harv's plot is Tsali Campground, where hikers, horseback riders, and especially mountain bikers congregate. These hearty adventurers catch their collective breath here at Tsali between excursions along the 39 miles of trails that emanate from the campground bordering Fontana Lake.

Tsali Campground is divided into two loops, an upper and a lower. The upper loop has 22 sites. The Forest Service keeps the campground well groomed, and plenty of second-growth hardwoods and pines shade the former field. A sparse understory makes the campground more open, yet sacrifices privacy. Six of the sites are spread along Mouse Branch. Four water spigots are evenly dispersed along the loop. In the loop's center sit a pair of low-volume flush toilets.

The lower loop features 19 sites and is more open and spacious than the upper loop, having fewer trees and, in some spots, a grassy understory. Eight sites back against Mouse Branch. At the head of the lower loop is a modern bath facility with flush toilets and hot showers, which are quite popular with sweaty hikers

RATINGS

Beauty: ✿ ✿ ✿ ✿
Privacy: ✿ ✿ ✿
Spaciousness: ✿ ✿ ✿
Quiet: ✿ ✿
Security: ✿ ✿ ✿ ✿ ✿
Cleanliness: ✿ ✿ ✿ ✿ ✿

and bikers. There are three water spigots conveniently located on the lower loop, where a short trail leads down to Fontana Lake.

The campground is full on weekends and busy during the week with active campers. Mountain bikers from all over the Southeast converge on Tsali to ride its trails. Many campers bring canoes as well, to drift on Fontana Lake and glide on the nearby white-water rivers. Hikers abound. Pleasure boaters and equestrians have their fair representation too.

There are four primary Tsali trails. The Forest Service has devised a system enabling all three groups—hikers, bikers, and equestrians—to enjoy the trails without bothering one another. Hikers can use all four trails at any time. The Right Loop and Left Loop trails are paired together. The Mouse Branch and Thompson Loop trails are paired together in a system whereby equestrians and bikers alternate daily use of the paired trails. The Right Loop Trail is a single-track trail that extends for 11 miles with views of Fontana Lake. It can be shortened to 4-or 8-mile loops. The Left Loop Trail is a 12-mile single-track pathway that features an overlook with a view of the Smoky Mountains. Mouse Branch Trail mixes a single-track trail with old logging roads and passes through old homesites along its 6-mile course. You may see wildlife on the 8-mile Thompson Loop Trail. It crosses streams and passes through wildlife openings and old homesites. Check the trail-use schedule posted at the campground.

The boat ramp presents more recreational opportunities. You can fish in Fontana Lake or access the Smokies. Cross the water and anchor in any cove on the Smokies' side of the lake. Then meander up the creek that created the cove and you will run into the Lakeshore Trail. It extends for miles in both directions. Many relics of the past may be seen, including stone walls, chimneys, and broken china. Make it an adventure. But remember, all artifacts are part of the park and must be left behind for others to enjoy.

Other facilities at Tsali include: a bike washing area for cleaning up after those long, muddy rides; a stable for horses; and a bank-fishing trail near the boat

KEY INFORMATION

ADDRESS:	Tsali Campground 1131 Massey Branch Road Robbinsville, NC 28771
OPERATED BY:	U.S. Forest Service
INFORMATION:	(828) 479-6431; www.cs.unca.edu/nfs nc
OPEN:	April 14–October 31
SITES:	41
EACH SITE HAS:	Tent pad, lantern post, picnic table, fire grate
ASSIGNMENT:	First come, first served; no reservations
REGISTRATION:	Self-registration on site
FACILITIES:	Water, flush toilets, hot shower
PARKING:	At campsites only
FEE:	$15 per night
ELEVATION:	1,750 feet
RESTRICTIONS:	**Pets:** On leash only **Fires:** In fire rings only **Alcohol:** At campsites only **Vehicles:** None **Other:** 14-day stay limit

MAP

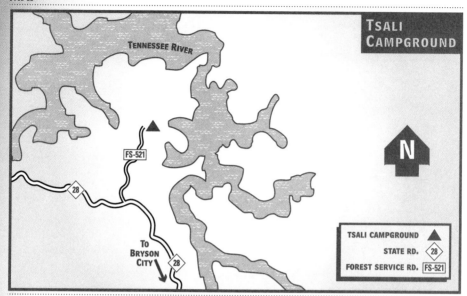

TSALI CAMPGROUND

TENNESSEE RIVER

FS-521

28

TO
BRYSON
CITY 28

N

TSALI CAMPGROUND	▲
STATE RD.	⟨28⟩
FOREST SERVICE RD.	FS-521

GETTING THERE

From Bryson City take US 19 south for 9 miles. Then turn right on NC 28 for 5.5 miles. Turn right again at the signed junction on FS 521 and follow it for 1.5 miles. Tsali Campground will be on your left.

launch for safely wetting a line. If you need supplies, drive west on NC 28 to Wolf Creek General Store.

This is a fun area for active people. Use Tsali as a base camp and enjoy any and all of the activities available in this beautiful section of the Southern Appalachians.

NORTH CAROLINA **PIEDMONT**

BADIN LAKE CAMPGROUND

DEPENDING ON WHERE you are coming from, there are several ways to reach Badin Lake Campground. Most of them take a lot of twists and turns, but the drive is worth it. This lakeside campground is the pride of the Uwharrie National Forest and it's a best bet for tent campers who want a quality campground accompanied by water and land recreation, including boating, fishing, and hiking. Maybe that's why it seems that all roads and signs in the Uwharrie National Forest lead to Badin Lake Campground.

This lakeside camp is broken into two loops. The Lower Loop has campsites 1 through 21. The terrain slopes toward Badin Lake, but the campsites themselves have been leveled with landscaping timbers. Some of these sites are multitiered. Pines reach high with cedars, oaks, sweetgum, and heavy brush below. The lakeside sites start with 4, which is a double site. Other double sites are 13, 20, and 22. If you are reserving a site and want a lakeside site, go for campsite 4, 6, 8, 9, 11, 12, or 13. These are single sites. The Lower Loop curves away from the lake and offers more attractive wooded sites.

On a hill overlooking the lake, the Upper Loop has sites 22 through 34. Sites 26 and 29 are closest to the water. This loop is lesser used and offers the most solitude. Being farther from Badin Lake makes it less popular. All sites are reservable, so crowding isn't a concern if you plan ahead. The sites are generally large and appear to be well-maintained. Heavy brush between sites offers more than adequate privacy. A campground host is on duty most of the year, providing an element of safety not found at unhosted campgrounds.

Badin Lake, covering 5,350 acres, is an impoundment of the Yadkin River. The eastern shore of the lake borders the national forest and is where the campground is located. Favored fish are bluegill, crappie,

> *Badin Lake offers water and land recreation in the Uwharrie Mountains.*

RATINGS

Beauty: ✩ ✩ ✩
Privacy: ✩ ✩ ✩ ✩
Spaciousness: ✩ ✩ ✩ ✩
Quiet: ✩ ✩ ✩
Security: ✩ ✩ ✩ ✩
Cleanliness: ✩ ✩ ✩

ADDRESS: Badin Lake
Campground
789 NC Hwy 24/27 E
Troy, NC 27371

OPERATED BY: U.S. Forest Service

INFORMATION: (910) 576-6391;
www.cs.unca.edu/nfs
nc/recreation/uwhar
rie/index; reserva-
tions, (877) 444-6777,
www.reserveusa.com

OPEN: Year-round

SITES: 34

EACH SITE HAS: Picnic table, fire
grate, tent pad,
lantern post

ASSIGNMENT: First come, first
served and by reser-
vation

REGISTRATION: Self-registration on
site

FACILITIES: Vault toilet, water
spigots

PARKING: At campsites only

FEE: $8 per night

ELEVATION: 525 feet

RESTRICTIONS: Pets: On leash only
Fires: In fire rings
only
Alcohol: No
Vehicles: None
Other: 14-day stay
limit

largemouth bass, catfish, and stripers. Anglers will be using worms and crickets with a bobber in spring for bluegill. Get on a bed of the slabsiders and you are in for some fun. Bass will be moving according to season. Try rocky points or around submerged logs. Crappie generally will go for minnows. Stripers are large bass and can be caught on live shad or top-water lures. Catfish are bottom feeders and will go for chicken livers or even a hot dog if kept on the lakebed with weights.

While others ski, swim (although no formal swimming area exists), and sun on the lake, campers with lakeside sites can enjoy the lake directly from their tents. For those with boats, Cove Boat Ramp is 2 miles from Badin Lake Campground, near Arrowhead Campground. Badin Lake Campground has a fishing pier nearby if you are boatless. Hikers can enjoy lakeside hiking directly from their campsite. A connector trail leads down to Badin Lake between campsite 9 and 11. From here, the Badin Lake Trail leads south along the shore to a shortcut loop and beyond, all the way south to Arrowhead Campground. The path then returns through the woods to the lake. Leave north from Badin Lake Campground and head over a ridge and along the shore to a north-facing point. Return through deep woods. The longer loop is 5.6 miles and the shortcut loop is 2.5 miles. You can hike to a remote spot and fish from shore or just look for wildlife, especially birds. Look also for old evidence of gold mining such as pits and tailings. Just realize your richest find here will be your campsite at Badin Lake Campground.

MAP

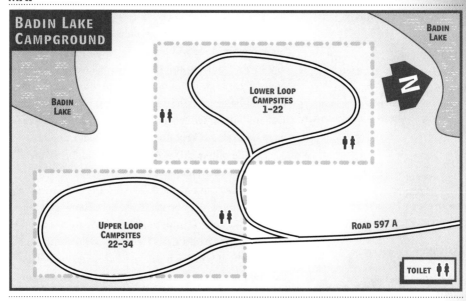

BADIN LAKE CAMPGROUND

BADIN LAKE

BADIN LAKE

LOWER LOOP CAMPSITES 1–22

UPPER LOOP CAMPSITES 22–34

ROAD 597 A

TOILET

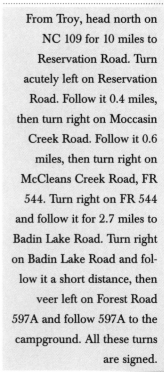

GETTING THERE

From Troy, head north on NC 109 for 10 miles to Reservation Road. Turn acutely left on Reservation Road. Follow it 0.4 miles, then turn right on Moccasin Creek Road. Follow it 0.6 miles, then turn right on McCleans Creek Road, FR 544. Turn right on FR 544 and follow it for 2.7 miles to Badin Lake Road. Turn right on Badin Lake Road and follow it a short distance, then veer left on Forest Road 597A and follow 597A to the campground. All these turns are signed.

HANGING ROCK
STATE PARK

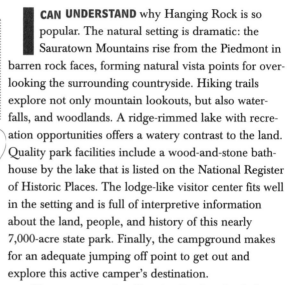

> *This state park is deservedly popular for its far-reaching vistas and tumbling cascades.*

I **CAN UNDERSTAND** why Hanging Rock is so popular. The natural setting is dramatic: the Sauratown Mountains rise from the Piedmont in barren rock faces, forming natural vista points for overlooking the surrounding countryside. Hiking trails explore not only mountain lookouts, but also waterfalls, and woodlands. A ridge-rimmed lake with recreation opportunities offers a watery contrast to the land. Quality park facilities include a wood-and-stone bathhouse by the lake that is listed on the National Register of Historic Places. The lodge-like visitor center fits well in the setting and is full of interpretive information about the land, people, and history of this nearly 7,000-acre state park. Finally, the campground makes for an adequate jumping off point to get out and explore this active camper's destination.

The campground at Hanging Rock is divided into two loops. The first loop has campsites 1 through 42 and is open throughout the week. Hickory, oaks, and maples shade the ridge-line campground that is slightly sloped. Sourwood, sassafras, and mountain laurel form a thick understory that screens the campsites from one another. Campsites are situated as the rocks and trees allow, resulting in campsites of differing sizes and distances from the loop. A trail leads down to the park lake, which is in the valley below the campground.

The second loop, with sites 43 through 73, is stretched on a ridge-line road. It is open only on weekends. The sites on the right side of the road are more desirable, as they face into the lake valley, rather than toward the campground access road. Mountains are visible beyond the lake through the trees. The campground road descends along the ridge, but the campsites themselves have been leveled. Be aware that these sites are closer together than the first loop.

RATINGS

Beauty: ✿ ✿ ✿ ✿
Privacy: ✿ ✿ ✿
Spaciousness: ✿ ✿
Quiet: ✿ ✿ ✿
Security: ✿ ✿ ✿ ✿ ✿
Cleanliness: ✿ ✿ ✿ ✿

Each loop has a bathhouse. Water spigots are adequately spread throughout the campground, which has a host to make your stay flow more smoothly. The only real downside to this park is campground popularity. It will fill just about every nice weekend. First come, first served means take your chances, but the campground host told me to get here by 1 p.m. on a Friday to get a site (my trip was on a weekday). Better yet, try to come during the week or mix your weekends and weekdays together if you can swing it.

Over 18 miles of trails travel to and through the park's natural features. The Hanging Rock Trail leads to the park's namesake. You can even see downtown Winston-Salem from Hanging Rock! Additional views await at other destinations. An observation tower has been erected at Moore's Knob. This is part of a fire tower from the state fire service. Check out the vistas from Cook's Wall, which leads to a cliff edge and House Rock. Other worthwhile hiking destinations are the Lower Cascades, Upper Cascades, Window Falls, and Hidden Falls. Haven't gotten enough falls? Then head to Tory's Falls. Here also is Tory's Den, a cave that was purportedly used during the Revolutionary War.

The park lake has a rustic bathhouse built by the Civilian Conservation Corps in the 1930s and early 1940s. A slope leads beyond the bathhouse to a beach, then to the clear lake itself, which was dammed by the CCC. This attractive impoundment offers fishing from a pier. Visitors can also rent paddleboats and rowboats to tool around the lake or angle for bream and bass. No private boats are allowed. The impressive park visitor center has an interesting video from the CCC days, among other information that is worth a visit. As pretty as the park structures may be, the natural landscape is the star of the show here. Make time to pitch your tent here, and check it out for yourself.

KEY INFORMATION

ADDRESS:	Hanging Rock State Park
	P.O. Box 278
	Danbury, NC 27016
OPERATED BY:	North Carolina State Parks
INFORMATION:	(336) 593-8480; www.ncsparks.net
OPEN:	Year-round
SITES:	73
EACH SITE HAS:	Picnic table, fire grate, tent pad
ASSIGNMENT:	First come, first served; no reservations
REGISTRATION:	Ranger will come by and register you
FACILITIES:	Hot shower, flush toilets, water spigot, bathhouse open March 15 through November, pit toilet only in winter
PARKING:	At campsites only
FEE:	$12 per night; $8 per night, winter
ELEVATION:	1,500 feet
RESTRICTIONS:	**Pets:** On leash only
	Fires: In fire rings only
	Alcohol: Prohibited
	Vehicles: Must be on parking pad
	Other: 14-day stay limit in a 30-day period

MAP

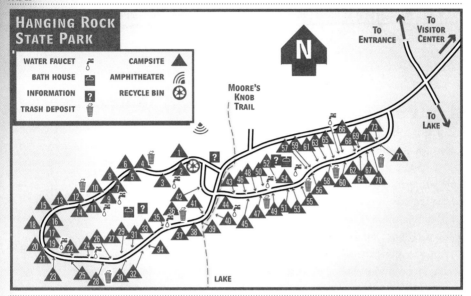

GETTING THERE

From Winston-Salem, take exit 110B from US 52, and take US 311 for 17 miles to NC 89. Keep forward on NC 89 west for 9 miles to Hanging Rock Road. Turn left on Hanging Rock Road and follow it for 1 mile to enter the state park.

LAKE NORMAN STATE PARK

WITH A NAME LIKE Lake Norman, it's pretty obvious this state park is a water-oriented destination. In that regard, it doesn't disappoint. Nearly the entire preserve is situated on a peninsula jutting into this impoundment, located just north of the greater Charlotte area. So it's no surprise the park campground is by the water, and the park has a swim area, boat launch, shore fishing, and a hiking trail that curves along the lake. And if that's not enough water, there's more—Lake Norman State Park has its own small lake where you can rent canoes and paddleboats and enjoy a smaller lake setting.

Once you arrive at the state park it seems to take forever to get to the actual campground. That is because the campground is at the tip of the peninsula that the state park owns. Having only 33 sites keeps the atmosphere relaxed, even when the campground is full, and that's just about every nice weekend between mid-April and Labor Day. Entering a loop with one cross road cutting the loop in half, the peninsula is hilly enough to offer vertical variation, but the campsites have been leveled. A tent pad at each site assures a level night's sleep. Many sites also have a leveled picnic-table pad, so the camp stew won't tip off your stove. A pretty forest of cedar, shortleaf pine, sourwood, and other hardwoods shades the campground. The forest is young, but thick, and offers good campsite privacy. Past the first three campsites, the main campground road continues curving along the lakeshore, while a crossroad leaves left. A connector hiking trail leaves the campground to meet the Lakeshore Trail across from campsite 3. Campsites 4, 5, and 6 are sloped downhill toward the lake and are heavily shaded. Campsite 12 is closest to the water but none of the sites are directly lakeside. Campsites 13 and 14 jut toward the water but are close to each other.

> *This state park offers the only publicly owne campground on Lake Norman.*

RATINGS

Beauty: ✿ ✿ ✿
Privacy: ✿ ✿ ✿ ✿
Spaciousness: ✿ ✿
Quiet: ✿ ✿
Security: ✿ ✿ ✿ ✿ ✿
Cleanliness: ✿ ✿ ✿

ADDRESS:	Lake Norman State Park
	159 Inland Sea Lane
	Troutman, NC 28166
OPERATED BY:	North Carolina State Parks
INFORMATION:	(704) 528-6350; www.ncsparks.net
OPEN:	March 15–November 30
SITES:	33
EACH SITE HAS:	Picnic table, fire ring, tent pad
ASSIGNMENT:	First come, first served; no reservations
REGISTRATION:	Ranger will come by and register you
FACILITIES:	Hot showers, flush toilets, water spigots
PARKING:	At campsites only
FEE:	$12 per night
ELEVATION:	800 feet
RESTRICTIONS:	**Pets:** On leash only
	Fires: In fire rings only
	Alcohol: Prohibited
	Vehicles: Car must fit on campsite drive up
	Other: 14-day stay limit

The lake views are gone by campsite 20. Campsite 23 and 24 offer good solitude. The campground crossroad has campsites 26 through 33, but the sites are a bit packed in. Campsite 31 is very near the bathhouse. The campground host stays on this crossroad.

A bathhouse centers the loop and is convenient to all campers. The campground as a whole is well maintained and appealing. Plan on getting a site by noon on Friday, during high summer. Weekdays aren't crowded but do get some interstate traffic from I-77.

As mentioned, this state park is centered on the water. The swim area on Lake Norman is popular during the summer. Boatless campers can fish from shore, or head up to the small park lake and rent a paddleboat or canoe and fish in a "no gas motors" atmosphere. Those with boats will use the park boat ramp to access Lake Norman for fishing, skiing, and general water recreation. If you want to be near the water, but not on the water, take the Lake Shore Trail. It meanders along most of the peninsula, which is bordered by Hicks Creek and the main lake. The entire loop is a 6.5-mile trek. Or take a shortcut on the Short Turn Trail and make your loop only 3.4 miles. The Alder Trail is much shorter at 0.8 miles. It is located at the park lake, where the rental boats are. This used to be a busier area when they had the swim beach here, but it now seems forgotten. Bicyclists love to pedal along the many park roads. The park even has a 3-mile mountain bike trail for those who want a little off-road pedaling action. And there is plenty of outdoor action here at Lake Norman State Park.

MAP

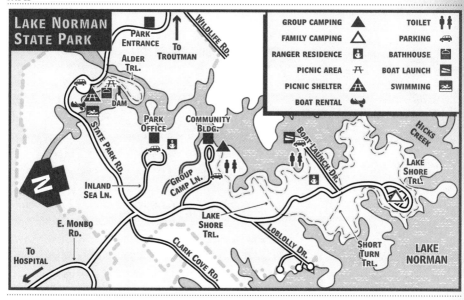

LAKE NORMAN STATE PARK

GROUP CAMPING	▲	TOILET	👫
FAMILY CAMPING	△	PARKING	🚗
RANGER RESIDENCE	🏠	BATHHOUSE	🚿
PICNIC AREA	🪑	BOAT LAUNCH	⛵
PICNIC SHELTER	⛺	SWIMMING	🏊
BOAT RENTAL	🛶		

PARK ENTRANCE — To TROUTMAN
ALDER TRL.
WILDLIFE RD.
DAM
STATE PARK RD.
PARK OFFICE
COMMUNITY BLDG.
BOAT LAUNCH DR.
HICKS CREEK
LAKE SHORE TRL.
INLAND SEA LN.
GROUP CAMP LN.
LAKE SHORE TRL.
E. MONBO RD.
LOBLOLLY DR.
To HOSPITAL
CLARK COVE RD.
SHORT TURN TRL.
LAKE NORMAN

GETTING THERE

From Exit 42 on I-77, just south of Statesville, take US 21 north for 2.7 miles to the town of Troutman. Take an acute left on Perth Road and follow Perth Road for 1.5 miles to State Park Road. Turn right on State Park Road and follow it for 2 miles to enter the state park.

MORROW MOUNTAIN
STATE PARK

> *This mountainous getaway on the Piedmont features hiking, boating, fishing, and swimming.*

THE PEAKS OF **MORROW MOUNTAIN** will surprise. They aren't the "big highs" of western Carolina, but if you want a touch and feel of the mountains without having to drive all the way to western Carolina come here. Relative to the terrain of the surrounding Piedmont, the Uwharrie Mountains rise to offer vertical relief and a mountain aura to the upper Pee Dee River valley. Back in the 1930s, local citizens noted the area's beauty and strove to develop a park. Today the 4,700-acre park offers a large quality campground, over 30 miles of trails, and water recreation on Lake Tillery, which is located at the base of the mountains.

Normally a campground with over 100 sites can resemble a mini "tent city." Morrow Mountain, however, bucks the trend. Three separate loops spread over a wide area, each with its own bathhouse, seem like three individual campgrounds rather than one oversized tent dealership. Loop A houses campsites 1 through 36 on a slight slope. A mix of pines, sweetgum, cedar, and understory trees such as dogwood shade the camps.

Loop B, featuring woodsy sites 37 through 68, is the most isolated and the most popular. It is located on a spur ridge with land dropping off on the outside of the loop, creating a mountain atmosphere. Where the slope is excessive, the campsites have been leveled. Try to get a site on the outside of the loop, as the sites there offer more space. Also, the sites are a bit closer together than on Loop A. Some sites have parking spurs that pull directly to the campsite while others necessitate a short walk to the camping area. The end of the loop backs against a narrow hollow, creating additional sloping.

Loop C was my choice, with sites 69 through 106. This loop is the most level, has campsites that are

RATINGS

Beauty: ✿ ✿ ✿ ✿
Privacy: ✿ ✿ ✿
Spaciousness: ✿ ✿ ✿ ✿ ✿
Quiet: ✿ ✿ ✿ ✿
Security: ✿ ✿ ✿ ✿ ✿
Cleanliness: ✿ ✿ ✿ ✿

more widespread than Loops A and B, and is the only loop open in winter. Bisected by a crossroad, some sites along this loop are very open and grassy, which is desirable during the colder months, while pines shade others. Younger hardwoods shade yet other sites. A campground host is here, except in winter, for your safety and convenience. Morrow Mountain will fill holiday weekends and a few ideal weather weekends during spring and fall.

When asked why campers come here, one park ranger summed it up in one word, "Variety." The state park offers both waterfront and mountaintop attractions. Lake Tillery, a 17-mile impoundment of the upper Pee Dee River, offers the water recreation. Campers with boats can use the park ramp to ply the lake, fishing for striped bass, largemouth bass, crappie, bream, and catfish. If you don't have a boat, you can rent canoes or rowboats for exploring the lake. Otherwise, use the 120-foot fishing pier. The park also has the only swimming pool in the North Carolina state park system. Open during the summer, the pool features a bathhouse constructed of native stone built in the 1930s.

The park's trail system stretches from one end of its boundaries to the other. Half the trails are hiker only and the other half are hiker/horse paths. The Rocks Trail leads directly from the campground to an outcrop overlooking Lake Tillery. The Hattaway Mountain Trail is less used and more challenging, offering winter vistas. Take the Sugarloaf Mountain Trail and the Morrow Mountain Trail for far reaching views of the lake and land beyond. Of course, a road leads to instant vistas atop Morrow Mountain. Speaking of roads, bicyclers like to pedal their way around the park; but be advised, some of these roads are steep.

Visitors should also explore the park's history, too. The Kron House is a homeplace reconstruction of the area's first doctor, Francis Kron. A home, office, infirmary, and greenhouse appear much as they did in the 1870s. Weekend interpretive programs tell of Kron's day and other aspects of the state park. You ought to take the good doctor's advice and settle down here for a spell. Bring your tent.

KEY INFORMATION

ADDRESS: Morrow Mountain State Park 49104 Morrow Mountain Road Albemarle, NC 28001

OPERATED BY: North Carolina State Parks

INFORMATION: (704) 982-4402; www.ncsparks.net

OPEN: Year-round; only C Loop open in winter

SITES: 106

EACH SITE HAS: Picnic table, fire grate, lantern post, tent pad

ASSIGNMENT: First come, first served; no reservations

REGISTRATION: Ranger will come by and register you

FACILITIES: Hot showers, flush toilets, water spigots

PARKING: At campsites only

FEE: $12 per night

ELEVATION: 450 feet

RESTRICTIONS: Pets: On leash only
Fires: In fire rings only
Alcohol: Prohibited
Vehicles: On designated parking pad
Other: 14-day stay limit in 30-day period

MAP

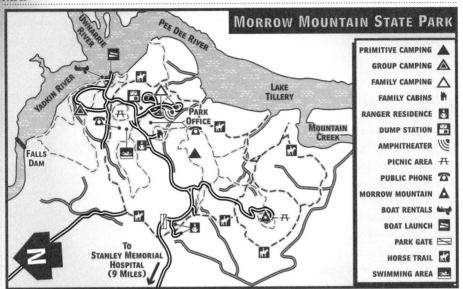

MORROW MOUNTAIN STATE PARK

PRIMITIVE CAMPING	▲
GROUP CAMPING	◬
FAMILY CAMPING	△
FAMILY CABINS	🏠
RANGER RESIDENCE	🏘
DUMP STATION	🚻
AMPHITHEATER	🔊
PICNIC AREA	🛖
PUBLIC PHONE	☎
MORROW MOUNTAIN	▲
BOAT RENTALS	🛶
BOAT LAUNCH	⬛
PARK GATE	⬔
HORSE TRAIL	🐎
SWIMMING AREA	🏊

GETTING THERE

From downtown Badin, take Falls Road for 0.1 mile to Boyden Street. Turn right on Boyden Street, staying left past the golf course and staying with it for a total of 2.4 miles to Morrow Mountain Road. Turn left on Morrow Mountain Road and follow it 1.5 miles to reach the park.

PILOT MOUNTAIN STATE PARK

NORTH CAROLINA HAS MANY special mountains, but as far as being a memorable and distinct landmark, Pilot Mountain takes the cake. Located on the edge of the Piedmont, Pilot Mountain rises from the surrounding lands to climax in a circular peak of nearly vertical rock walls with a wooded cap. Named Pilot Mountain for its status as a way marker for all who passed by, the park is now a great destination for tent campers. Hiking and rock climbing are the primary past times here. The mountain area of the park is complemented with an additional state park segment on the Yadkin River, which has a living historical farm, fishing and canoeing opportunities, and hiking trails.

The campground is situated, not surprisingly, on a slope of Pilot Mountain. Before you imagine having to buckle yourself in from rolling off a hill, realize that the sites themselves have been leveled—for the most part—but all sites have level tent pads, making mountainside slumber more likely.

The paved campground loop has paved parking spurs to minimize erosion and keep your car from sliding off the mountain. Overhead, chestnut oaks, dogwoods, and hickory shade the camps. Mountain laurel and young trees make a passable understory. Many of the campsites are separated from the parking spur, necessitating a short walk into the woods and sometimes up or down steps. This short walk actually increases campsite privacy. The fitting in of campsites where the terrain allows compromises campsite size. Most are average in size, while others are small. Limiting your gear will increase your site choices. Cruise around the loop, passing the Grindstone Trail beyond campsite 16. A modern bathhouse stands near campsite 25. From here, the loop circles downhill. Sometimes, a site's picnic table and tent pad are a bit apart,

> *Pilot Mountain is a North Carolina landmark.*

RATINGS

Beauty: ☆ ☆ ☆ ☆
Privacy: ☆ ☆ ☆
Spaciousness: ☆ ☆
Quiet: ☆ ☆ ☆ ☆
Security: ☆ ☆ ☆ ☆ ☆
Cleanliness: ☆ ☆ ☆

ADDRESS:	Pilot Mountain State Park
	1792 Pilot Knob Park Road
	Pinnacle, NC 27699
OPERATED BY:	North Carolina State Parks
INFORMATION:	(336) 325-2355; www.ncsparks.net
OPEN:	March 15–November 30
SITES:	49
EACH SITE HAS:	Picnic table, fire ring, tent pad,
ASSIGNMENT:	First come first served; no reservations
REGISTRATION:	Ranger will come by and register you
FACILITIES:	Hot showers, flush toilets, water spigots
PARKING:	At campsites only
FEE:	$12 per night
ELEVATION:	1,000 feet
RESTRICTIONS:	**Pets:** On leash only
	Fires: In fire rings only
	Alcohol: Prohibited
	Vehicles: 32-foot trailer limit
	Other: 14-day stay limit in 30-day period

due to terrain. However, the sloping mountainside enhances the camping atmosphere here on Pilot Mountain, where 95% of the campsites are desirable.

Weekdays are very quiet and, surprisingly, Pilot Mountain fills only on holiday weekends. Other than then you should get a site. You will be sharing the campground with young couples, families, the occasional rock climber, and other folks who come here to get a first-hand look at the unusual mountain.

The view looking up at Pilot Mountain as you arrive arouses a curiosity to see what it's like looking down on the surrounding landscape. Here are the statistics: Pilot Mountain stands 2,421 feet in elevation, more than 1,400 feet above the surrounding countryside. On a clear day you can see over 3,000 square miles from the Little Pinnacle Overlook.

More than 27 miles of trails course through the mountain section of the park and the river section combined. The Jomeokee Trail circles the crest of the circular mountain. The Grindstone Trail leads from the campground and allows access to the other high country paths. The longest trail is the Corridor Trail, which connects the river and mountain sections of the park together. The river section of the park is centered on the Yadkin Islands, on the Yadkin River. The Horne Creek Trail starts near the Horne Creek Living Historical Farm, where on weekends, folks dressed in 1900 period clothes go about the business of farm life from that era. Check ahead with the park to make sure a demonstration is going on during your visit. The nearby Yadkin River offers 165 miles of canoeing possibilities. The Shoals Access site is just upstream of the Yadkin Islands. Your watery river experience should contrast well with your more solid explorations from atop Pilot Mountain.

MAP

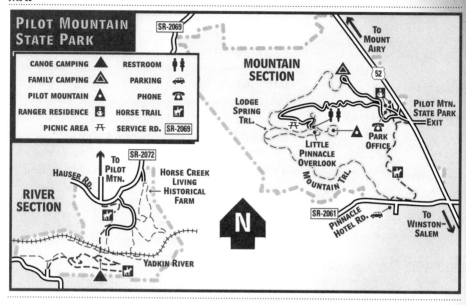

PILOT MOUNTAIN STATE PARK

CANOE CAMPING	▲	RESTROOM	👫
FAMILY CAMPING	⛺	PARKING	🚗
PILOT MOUNTAIN	⛺	PHONE	☎
RANGER RESIDENCE		HORSE TRAIL	
PICNIC AREA	🪵	SERVICE RD.	SR-2069

SR-2069

MOUNTAIN SECTION

To MOUNT AIRY

52

PILOT MTN. STATE PARK EXIT

LODGE SPRING TRL.

PARK OFFICE

LITTLE PINNACLE OVERLOOK

MOUNTAIN TRL.

To PILOT MTN.

SR-2072

HAUSER RD.

RIVER SECTION

HORSE CREEK LIVING HISTORICAL FARM

N

SR-2061

PINNACLE HOTEL RD.

To WINSTON-SALEM

YADKIN RIVER

GETTING THERE

From Winston-Salem, drive north on US 52 and take the Pilot Mountain exit, a non-numbered exit. (The Pilot Mountain exit is the next exit after Exit 129 for the town of Pinnacle.) Turn left on Pilot Mountain Road and follow it 1 mile to the park, on your left.

WEST MORRIS MOUNTAIN CAMPGROUND

> *This off-the-beaten-path campground offers access to the lesser-used Uwharrie Trail.*

MY EXPECTATIONS WERE LOW before arriving at West Morris Mountain Campground. Most of the smaller recreation destinations of the Uwharrie National Forest had been broken-down hunt camps. I was hoping against hope for something good, and my hopes were realized on this ridge top. The campground was in great shape! And the master path of this national forest, the Uwharrie Trail, ran a single mile distant from the campground. Furthermore, a side trail connected West Morris Mountain to the Uwharrie Trail!

The mountains of the Uwharrie are not like the mountains of western Carolina, but they do offer distinct topographical relief, a milder climate, and much easier access from the Piedmont than the Appalachians to the west. Elevations generally range from 400 to 900 feet, and the crowd numbers are much lower here as well. Although lacking the vertical height of other North Carolina mountains, this area has its beauty. My fall tour of the Uwharries was well timed. The yellow sugar maples and red dogwoods were bursting with color contrasting against a cobalt blue sky. That nip in the air offered brisk relief from the long, hot summer.

The campground is set on the western shoulder of Morris Mountain. Pass a few sites that do have tent pads and are in a mix of grass and woods before entering the main campground. These sites have not been numbered in the past but are considered campsites and may be numbered by the time you get here. The main campground is strung out on a classic loop. The sites have been rehabilitated and are in good shape. A hardwood forest of maples, oaks, and dogwoods with assorted pines shades the campsites. Heavy vegetation screens the campsites from one another. Campsite 1 is on the loop's inside. Campsite 2 offers privacy. Campsite 3 is away from the loop. Campsite 5 is next to a

RATINGS

Beauty: ✿ ✿ ✿ ✿
Privacy: ✿ ✿ ✿ ✿
Spaciousness: ✿ ✿ ✿
Quiet: ✿ ✿ ✿ ✿
Security: ✿ ✿
Cleanliness: ✿ ✿ ✿

modern vault toilet. Campsites 6 and 7 are heavily shaded. Campsite 8 is larger than most. Campsite 9 and 10 are on the outside of the loop and overlook a hollow. Campsite 11, 12, and 13 will suit most campers. Campsite 14 is a handicapped site. A second vault toilet is near here. Bring your own drinking water.

The sites are well spaced from one another but are small to average in size, which is good for tent campers since it discourages bigger rigs. Realistically, West Morris Mountain is too primitive for the non-tent camping set. This campground never fills.

The Morris Mountain Trail lies near the loop's beginning. Pass around a metal gate and begin climbing, to reach the Uwharrie Trail after 0.75 miles. Here the Uwharrie Trail leaves right and continues forward on the old roadbed. Joe Moffitt, who grew up in the Uwharrie Mountains, built the 21-mile Uwharrie Trail. It passes over ridges, into streambeds, and passes old homesites and cemeteries. Unfortunately, loops are not possible in the northern end of the forest near West Morris Mountain. However, the 9.5-mile Dutchman's Creek Trail loops with the Uwharrie Trail in the south end of the forest.

The Birkhead Mountains Wilderness is not far from West Morris Mountain. This 5,000-acre preserve has stands of old-growth hardwoods broken by clear streams. Parts of it were settled and you can still see remnants of homesites and even gold mining operations. The wilderness trailhead can be reached by turning right out of the campground and staying on Ophir Road as it becomes Burney Mill Road, where you cross into Randolph County. Continue on to the intersection of Lassiter Mill Road and turn right. Keep north on Lassiter Mill Road and look for the trailhead on your right. A wilderness map is available from the ranger station in Troy, as is a Uwharrie Trail map. Order a forest map then discover the lesser-known Uwharrie Mountains.

KEY INFORMATION

ADDRESS: West Morris Mountain Campground 789 NC Hwy 24/27 E Troy, NC 27371

OPERATED BY: U.S. Forest Service

INFORMATION: (910) 576-6391; www.cs.unca.edu/nfs nc/recreation/ uwharrie/index

OPEN: Year-round

SITES: 17

EACH SITE HAS: Picnic table, fire grate, lantern post, tent pad

ASSIGNMENT: First come, first served; no reservations

REGISTRATION: Self-registration on-site

FACILITIES: Vault toilet

PARKING: At campsites only

FEE: $5 per night

ELEVATION: 450 feet

RESTRICTIONS: Pets: On leash only
Fires: In fire rings only
Alcohol: Prohibited
Vehicles: None
Other: Pack it in, pack it out

MAP

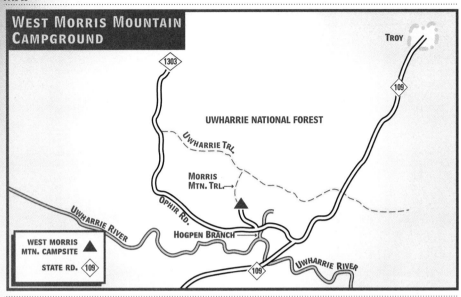

WEST MORRIS MOUNTAIN CAMPGROUND

TROY

1303

109

UWHARRIE NATIONAL FOREST

UWHARRIE TRL.

MORRIS MTN. TRL.

OPHIR RD.

UWHARRIE RIVER

HOGPEN BRANCH

WEST MORRIS MTN. CAMPSITE

STATE RD. 109

109

UWHARRIE RIVER

GETTING THERE

From Troy, head north on NC 109 for 9 miles to Ophir Road, NC 1303. Turn right on Ophir Road and follow it for 1 mile to the campground, on your right.

NORTH CAROLINA
COAST AND COASTAL PLAIN

CAROLINA BEACH
STATE PARK

THIS AREA OF THE CAROLINAS certainly has some amazing natural attributes, but the most unusual of all may be the Venus flytrap. Perhaps you have heard of it. The modified leaves of this plant close rapidly when an insect touches tiny hairs on the leaf's inside, trapping the insect, which then becomes dinner. This unusual plant grows only on land located within a 60-mile radius of Wilmington, North Carolina. Carolina Beach State Park has a trail where you can see this unusual plant. The park also has a fine, lesser-used campground as well as many attractions within a 10-mile radius of the campground, such as beaches, historic sites, and even an aquarium.

With all there is to do here, you should find the campground very appealing as a base camp. It is located in piney woods near Snows Cut, a waterway connecting the wide Cape Fear River to the Intracoastal Waterway. Pine trees tower over the two campground loops. Live oaks, water oaks, and other hardwoods are mixed in with the pines. Clumpy brush grows here and there among the woods, adding privacy. A drive on the paved campground road through the first loop will reveal large sites with a sand and pine-needle floor. The Snow's Cut Trail leads toward a maritime forest near campsite 21. We enjoyed campsite 25, where the filtering sunlight helped dry our gear after a storm pushed through the previous night. A bathhouse centers the loop. A short road with large campsites along it leads to the second loop. This second loop, with sites 48 through 82, is opened only when the first loop fills. The sites look little used in the second loop, but the first loop doesn't get a whole lot of business itself. The second loop, where the Sugarloaf Trail leaves from campsite 54, also has large campsites and a bathhouse in the center.

> *Many attractions are within a short drive of this lesser-used oceanside campground.*

RATINGS

Beauty: ✿ ✿ ✿ ✿
Privacy: ✿ ✿ ✿
Spaciousness: ✿ ✿ ✿ ✿
Quiet: ✿ ✿ ✿
Security: ✿ ✿ ✿ ✿ ✿
Cleanliness: ✿ ✿ ✿

KEY INFORMATION

ADDRESS: Carolina Beach State Park
P.O. Box 475
Carolina Beach, NC 28428

OPERATED BY: North Carolina State Parks

INFORMATION: (910) 458-8206;
www.ncparks.net

OPEN: Year-round

SITES: 83

EACH SITE HAS: Picnic table, fire ring

ASSIGNMENT: First come, first served; no reservations

REGISTRATION: At park store and marina

FACILITIES: Hot showers, flush toilets, water spigots

PARKING: At campsites only

FEE: $12 per night

ELEVATION: 10 feet

RESTRICTIONS: **Pets:** On leash only
Fires: In fire rings only
Alcohol: Prohibited
Vehicles: Two per site
Other: 6 campers per site

This park has an unusual system of claiming campsites. A little green tag hangs below each unoccupied and numbered campsite post. When you find a campsite you like, grab the green tag and take it to the park store and marina, then register there. The campground will fill most weekends from Memorial Day through Fourth of July weekend. After that, the heat keeps most campers away until fall, when cooler-weather weekends will become busy, but usually not full. A campsite can be had most spring weekends and anytime during winter. We came during fall—the weather was ideal and the insects weren't bothersome.

There are beach accesses aplenty near Carolina Beach Sate Park on nearby Pleasure Island. I recommend driving 5 miles to Fort Fisher State Recreation Area. It features 7 miles of state-owned beach with summer lifeguards in the designated ocean swimming area. Four-wheel-drive vehicles can access other areas along the beach. The recreation area is popular with beachcombers. The North Carolina Aquarium at Fort Fisher is a great place to check out marine life up close, and Fort Fisher State Historic Site is located nearby, where you can learn about the history of this Confederate Civil War bunker. Many folks like to tour the *USS North Carolina* battleship that is conspicuously located in the Cape Fear River near Wilmington.

Don't forget, though, about all the fun stuff to do at Carolina Beach State Park! The area is laced with hiking trails that crisscross numerous natural communities. The Fly Trap Trail features the famous Venus flytrap. The Sugarloaf Trail passes through tidal flat and pine woods. The Snows Cut Trail leads to the Intracoastal Waterway. The above 6 miles of trails are mostly hiked during cooler months.

For anglers, a fishing deck leading into the Cape Fear River is located near the park marina. This location attracts fishermen in all types of weather, going for croaker, flounder, and striped bass. The marina sells plenty of bait and tackle. Campers with boats will enjoy the convenience of the boat launch at the marina.

With an abundance of recreational and sightseeing opportunities close by, camping at Carolina Beach is pleasurable as well as convenient.

MAP

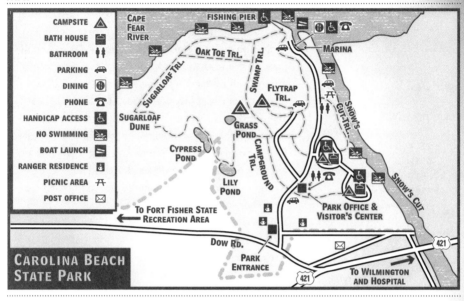

CAROLINA BEACH STATE PARK

Legend	
CAMPSITE	△
BATH HOUSE	🛁
BATHROOM	👥
PARKING	🚗
DINING	🍽
PHONE	☎
HANDICAP ACCESS	♿
NO SWIMMING	🚫
BOAT LAUNCH	🚤
RANGER RESIDENCE	🏠
PICNIC AREA	🎋
POST OFFICE	✉

CAPE FEAR RIVER

FISHING PIER

MARINA

OAK TOE TRL.

SUGARLOAF TRL.

SWAMP TRL.

FLYTRAP TRL.

SUGARLOAF DUNE

GRASS POND

CAMPGROUND TRL.

SNOW'S CUT-TRL.

SNOW'S CUT

CYPRESS POND

LILY POND

To FORT FISHER STATE RECREATION AREA ←

PARK OFFICE & VISITOR'S CENTER

DOW RD.

PARK ENTRANCE

421

To WILMINGTON AND HOSPITAL

GETTING THERE

From Wilmington, drive south on US 421 for 15 miles, crossing the Intracoastal Waterway. Turn right on Dow Road past the Intracoastal Waterway, shortly reaching the park, on your right.

CLIFFS OF THE NEUSE STATE PARK

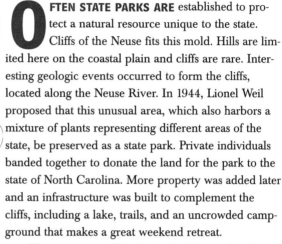

> *This underutilized campground stands next to some surprising terrain on the coastal plain.*

OFTEN STATE PARKS ARE established to protect a natural resource unique to the state. Cliffs of the Neuse fits this mold. Hills are limited here on the coastal plain and cliffs are rare. Interesting geologic events occurred to form the cliffs, located along the Neuse River. In 1944, Lionel Weil proposed that this unusual area, which also harbors a mixture of plants representing different areas of the state, be preserved as a state park. Private individuals banded together to donate the land for the park to the state of North Carolina. More property was added later and an infrastructure was built to complement the cliffs, including a lake, trails, and an uncrowded campground that makes a great weekend retreat.

The campground lies beneath rich woodland on slightly sloping land. Tall pines mix with a variety of hardwoods, including hickory, beech, and water oak. The brushy understory of holly, young sweetgum and other small trees can be thick in one spot and open in another, creating privacy at one campsite and openness at the next. The first few campsites are wooded around the edges and open in the center. Pine needles and sand carpet the campsites. I enjoyed campsite 12, because it shaded a strong September sun. Luckily, a cool night followed.

Barefoot campers should note campsite 14, as a holly tree stands in its center. Those prickly leaves might be hard on the feet. The loop curves around and reaches an area with limited shade starting at campsite 20. Thick brush shields the campsites on their sides, but are open overhead. Lush grass carpets these campsites, which show less use than the shaded sites. Thick woods resume past campsite 25. The loop curves uphill, making the last few campsites a bit too sloped for the best camping.

RATINGS

Beauty: ✪ ✪ ✪
Privacy: ✪ ✪ ✪
Spaciousness: ✪ ✪ ✪ ✪
Quiet: ✪ ✪ ✪ ✪
Security: ✪ ✪ ✪ ✪ ✪
Cleanliness: ✪ ✪ ✪

Overall, the campsites are large and desirable for tent campers, making the light usage of this campground surprising. It only fills on holiday weekends, so Cliffs of the Neuse is great for avoiding the crowds at other times, especially during spring and fall. Ideal weather weekends during these seasons only fill half the 35 sites.

Water spigots are laid out at convenient intervals along the loop. The bathhouse is accessed by trails spoking into the center of the loop. For your safety, the park gates are locked every night. If an emergency occurs, use the emergency number posted at the park office near the campground. Rangers live on-site and will assist you. The combination of locked gates and on-site rangers makes camping here a very safe endeavor.

An emergency may be the only time you have to get in your car while at the park. Access to all park facilities is just a walk away. For example, a trail leads from the campground to the park museum. Here, the formation of the Cliffs of the Neuse is explained in a manner that even the "geologically challenged" like me can understand. Park history is detailed as well. The actual Cliffs of the Neuse stand just feet from the museum. Go ahead and walk along the split-rail fence to garner some views that are unusual for this region, while the Neuse Rivers beckons below. Take the "350 Yard Trail" along the cliff to the river's edge. Here, anglers may be lazing away the day, going for large-mouth bass but more likely catching bream and bluegill. Gurgling Mill Creek is within earshot. The trail bridges Mill Creek where a facility for grinding corn once stood. The Galax Trail starts across the water. This is an isolated pocket of the galax plant, normally a mountain species of ground cover. The Bird Trail loops along the Neuse River, providing more bank-fishing opportunities there as well as along Still Creek, where whiskey was once made. These trails are great for families with kids or folks that just want a light leg stretcher.

Seeing the Neuse River made me want to go on a float trip. Conveniently, a shuttle and canoe livery service is located on the Neuse River near the park. The most popular run is from the NC 111 bridge down to the

MAP

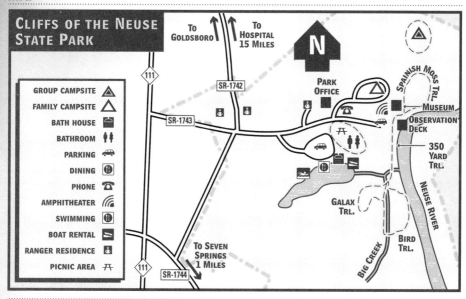

CLIFFS OF THE NEUSE STATE PARK

To GOLDSBORO
To HOSPITAL 15 MILES

N

111
SR-1742
SR-1743
111
SR-1744

GROUP CAMPSITE △
FAMILY CAMPSITE △
BATH HOUSE
BATHROOM
PARKING
DINING
PHONE ☎
AMPHITHEATER
SWIMMING
BOAT RENTAL
RANGER RESIDENCE
PICNIC AREA 𝝑

PARK OFFICE

MUSEUM
OBSERVATION DECK
350 YARD TRL.

SPANISH MOSS TRL.

GALAX TRL.

NEUSE RIVER

BIRD TRL.

BIG CREEK

To SEVEN SPRINGS 1 MILES

GETTING THERE

From Goldsboro, drive east on US 70 for 5 miles to NC 111. Turn right on NC 111 and follow it for 9 miles to Park Entrance Road. Turn left on Park Entrance Road and follow it into the park.

hamlet of Seven Springs, making a distance of 8 miles. The outfitter can be reached at (919) 734-2291.

The state park offers water recreations of its own. The upper reaches of Mill Creek have been dammed, forming a spring-fed, 11-acre lake. An elaborate swim area has been built, with a wide swim beach adjacent to a large grassy lawn. A changing building and snack bar are also located here. As you have read, the unique features that are the Cliffs of the Neuse have been protected and enhanced by this state park. Now, come check them out for yourself.

FRISCO CAMPGROUND

FRISCO **C**AMPGROUND **OFFERS** some phenomenal oceanside scenery. Located in the Cape Hatteras National Seashore, the campground is overlain on a series of dunes so hilly you might think you were in the mountains of North Carolina instead of the beach. OK, that is an exaggeration. However, oceanside topography doesn't get much more vertical than this in the Tar Heel State. Beach activities such as surf fishing, beachcombing, kayaking, and visiting lighthouses are on the agenda. Or maybe the agenda is to just sit by the Atlantic Ocean and listen to the waves roll in.

But make no mistake about it; this oceanside environment is harsh and unforgiving. That is what delivers the stark beauty that is the Outer Banks—a relentless ocean pounding against the sand, rolling dunes where sea oats cling to life, wind sculpted trees growing in dune swales, a strong sun beating down on the very openness that are the banks. The campground reflects this stark beauty. The sites themselves are appealing, but they are exposed to wind, sun, and mosquitoes.

The campground is laid out in a big loop with six roads crossing the loop. The loop is overlain a series of dunes, ever increasing in height as you head away from the ocean. The ocean runs parallel to the campground and is about 150 yards distant. Scattered cedars, oaks, and pines mostly grow brushy, looking nothing like you would see on the mainland. The wind keeps these trees from growing straight and tall. The trees are most stunted, if they can grow there at all, on the tops of dunes. In the swales, where the wind is less, the trees more resemble their inland cousins. But trees that grow over a person's head are few. Nevertheless, campsites with even a modicum of shade will be snapped up. Most sites are completely in the open, cutting campsite privacy to a minimum.

> *Pitch your tent among the rolling dunes of Cape Hatteras National Seashore.*

RATINGS

Beauty: ✪ ✪ ✪ ✪ ✪
Privacy: ✪
Spaciousness: ✪ ✪
Quiet: ✪ ✪ ✪ ✪
Security: ✪ ✪ ✪ ✪ ✪
Cleanliness: ✪ ✪

KEY INFORMATION

ADDRESS:	Frisco Campground Route 1, Box 675 Manteo, NC 27954
OPERATED BY:	National Park Service
INFORMATION:	(252) 473-2111; www.nps.gov/caha
OPEN:	Friday of Easter weekend through mid-October
SITES:	127
EACH SITE HAS:	Picnic table, upright grill
ASSIGNMENT:	First come, first served; no reservations
REGISTRATION:	At campground entrance booth
FACILITIES:	Cold showers, water spigots, flush toilets
PARKING:	At campsites only
FEE:	$18 per night
ELEVATION:	50 feet
RESTRICTIONS:	Pets: On leash only Fires: In upright grills only, below high tide line on beach Alcohol: At campsites only Vehicles: Two per site Other: All vehicles must be on paved parking surface

As the main loop curves around, pass some pine trees in the low area between the campground and the beach, which is accessed by two boardwalks. The road rises remarkably high, maybe a couple of hundred feet. These sites on the back of the loop begin to overlook the ocean, and offer stunning panoramas. Just like any site here, it has its pluses and minuses. The open sites will have the wind, which cuts down on mosquitoes, but if the wind is cold, then the openness is a negative. If the sun is blaring down, as it often is, then the lack of shade can be wearing. Bringing a screen shelter can eliminate both the sun and bug problems. Many sites are small, so you will have to be flexible in setting up your site. I stayed in site P 56 and enjoyed the afternoon shade, but the mosquitoes were a bit troublesome.

Campers usually end up finding a site to suit them. Do some driving around in the campground once you get here. No matter your location in this large campground, a bathhouse and water spigot are close by. Frisco will fill on major holidays and a few other assorted perfect weather weekends in summer. Otherwise, you should be able to get a campsite.

Four-wheel-drive vehicles can access the beach at many areas of Cape Hatteras National Seashore. These access points are referred to as "ramps," and one of these ramps is located adjacent to the campground. Most campers just use the boardwalks to reach the beach by foot. In either case, you have miles of shoreline to enjoy, whether you are surf casting or surfing with a board. A fishing pier is just west of the campground, as is a designated swim beach with a bathhouse.

Cape Hatteras Lighthouse is just a short drive away. It made the news some years ago when it was moved to keep it from falling into the shifting sea. You can climb this lighthouse and get a grand view, or walk the nearby Buxton Woods Trail, which is operated in conjunction with the Nature Conservancy. Supplies can be had in the village of Frisco, which is conveniently just a mile from the campground. And after staying a night or two, a mile may be all you will want to get away from here.

MAP

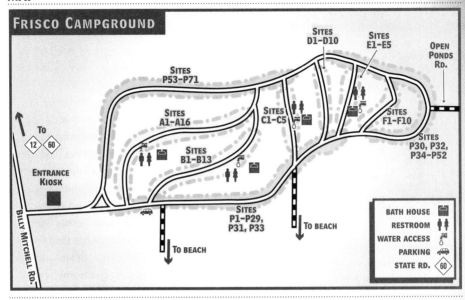

FRISCO CAMPGROUND

SITES D1–D10

SITES E1–E5

OPEN PONDS RD.

SITES P53–P71

SITES A1–A16

SITES C1–C5

SITES F1–F10

TO
12 60

ENTRANCE KIOSK

SITES B1–B13

SITES P30, P32, P34–P52

BILLY MITCHELL RD.

SITES P1–P29, P31, P33

TO BEACH

TO BEACH

BATH HOUSE	
RESTROOM	
WATER ACCESS	
PARKING	
STATE RD.	60

GETTING THERE

From the intersection of US 64/264 and US 158 just south of Nags Head, drive south on NC 12 for 60 miles to the hamlet of Frisco. Turn left on Billy Mitchell Road and follow it for 1 mile to reach the campground.

GOOSE CREEK
STATE PARK

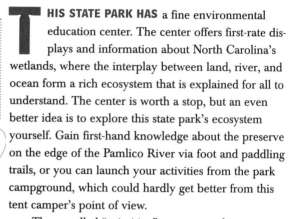

> *Enjoy some of the coastal plain's finest wetlands at this quiet state park.*

THIS STATE PARK HAS a fine environmental education center. The center offers first-rate displays and information about North Carolina's wetlands, where the interplay between land, river, and ocean form a rich ecosystem that is explained for all to understand. The center is worth a stop, but an even better idea is to explore this state park's ecosystem yourself. Gain first-hand knowledge about the preserve on the edge of the Pamlico River via foot and paddling trails, or you can launch your activities from the park campground, which could hardly get better from this tent camper's point of view.

The so-called "primitive" campground is set on a piece of high ground between Flatty Creek and Goose Creek. A narrow, gravel road stretches out beneath tall loblolly pines, complemented by hickory, oak, holly, and bay trees. The forest understory is light. Be careful driving the campground road, as trees grow so close alongside it that you might nick one with your car. A sign at the beginning of the campground states "No large RVs." Soon come to campsite 1. A gravel parking spur leads to a large campsite shaded by pine, oaks, and holly. Just like the other sites, one part of the campsite is sand to place your tent. I chose campsite 1. It was so alluring, I claimed it immediately without looking at the rest of the campground. But there are many other quality sites. Campsite 2 is a good 75 yards down the road. The sites here are as widespread as you are going to get. Campsite 2 has a gravel parking pad with a short walkway to reach the campsite. Most campsites here require a short walk to reach the actual camping area. Past 1 of 4 water spigots, campsite 3 is a double site, 200 feet from the road. Campsite 4 is a drive-up site. Across from site 4 is one of two composting toilets using the latest ventilation technology, which does make a difference in the odor department.

RATINGS

Beauty: ✿ ✿ ✿ ✿
Privacy: ✿ ✿ ✿ ✿ ✿
Spaciousness: ✿ ✿ ✿ ✿ ✿
Quiet: ✿ ✿ ✿ ✿ ✿
Security: ✿ ✿ ✿ ✿ ✿
Cleanliness: ✿ ✿ ✿ ✿ ✿

Keep going down the road. Campsite 5 is also a drive-up site. It has an upright grill in addition to a fire ring. Campsite 6 is a walk-in site to a shady flat. All the campsites here are level. Campsite 7 is on the right, across the road from the Flatty Creek Trail. Campsite 8 is a walk-in site scattered with pines. Campsite 9 is a walk-in site with a short walk. Designated parking spots are provided for each walk-in site. Campsite 10 has many hardwoods shading it. The last two campsites, 11 and 12, require a longer walk, but are also closest to Goose Creek. Campsite 12 looks toward water on three sides, though the water is a good 100 feet distant. An auto turnaround is at the end of the road, along with an observation deck that stretches into Goose Creek.

Spring and fall are the best time to camp at Goose Creek Campground. The campground will fill a couple of great weather weekends per season. A site will be available anytime of the year during the week, although summer is too hot and buggy.

Now, to explore the wetlands that make Goose Creek so special. You may want to visit the environmental education center first, to gain an understanding of the ecosystem and know what to look for, then take off. The Palmetto Boardwalk behind the nature center offers interpretive signage showing you the wetlands first hand. Campers can use the small sandy shore at the campground's edge to launch their canoe or kayak into the water. Here, you can join the Goose Creek Canoe Trail. It explores not only the natural history of the area, but also the human history. You can check out relics of an old logging operation in addition to wildflowers and wildlife, especially birds. Flatty Creek and Mallard Creek are also good paddling destinations, as is the shoreline along Pamlico River. The brackish river supports both salt and freshwater species, so bring your pole and angle for flounder, bream, black drum, and largemouth bass. A swim beach, requiring a short walk, is located on the Pamlico River, too.

Landlubbers have choices as well. The Ivey Gut Trail leaves from the upper end of the campground and curves alongside Goose Creek for a 2-mile, one-way trek. The Flatty Creek Trail is also accessible directly

KEY INFORMATION

ADDRESS: Goose Creek State Park
2190 Camp Leach Road
Washington, NC 27889

OPERATED BY: North Carolina State Parks

INFORMATION: (252) 923-0052; www.ncsparks.net

OPEN: Year-round

SITES: 12

EACH SITE HAS: Picnic table, fire ring, lantern post

ASSIGNMENT: First come, first served; no reservations

REGISTRATION: Ranger will come by and register you

FACILITIES: Water spigot, vault toilet

PARKING: At campsites only

FEE: $8 per night

ELEVATION: 10 feet

RESTRICTIONS: Pets: On leash only
Fires: In fire rings only
Alcohol: Prohibited
Vehicles: None
Other: 14-day stay limit in 30-day period

MAP

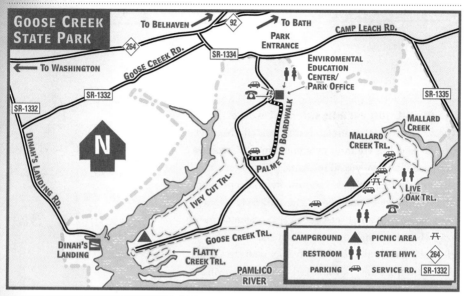

GOOSE CREEK STATE PARK

To Belhaven
92
To Bath
Park Entrance
Camp Leach Rd.
264
Goose Creek Rd.
SR-1334
To Washington
Enviromental Education Center/ Park Office
SR-1332
SR-1335
SR-1332
Mallard Creek
Mallard Creek Trl.
N
Palmetto Boardwalk
Live Oak Trl.
Ivey Cut Trl.
Dinah's Landing Rd.
Dinah's Landing
Goose Creek Trl.
Flatty Creek Trl.
Pamlico River

CAMPGROUND	▲	PICNIC AREA	⛱
RESTROOM	🚻	STATE HWY.	264
PARKING	🚗	SERVICE RD.	SR-1332

GETTING THERE

From Washington, head east on US 264 for 9 miles to Camp Leach Road. Turn right on Camp Leach Road and follow it 2.2 miles to the park.

from the campground. It makes a 1-mile loop through the woods and across boardwalks to reach an observation deck along Flatty Creek. The Goose Creek Trail is the park's longest at 2.9 miles. Here, you can enjoy some of the park's three types of primary wetlands— hardwood swamp, cypress gum swamp, and brackish marsh. The Ragged Point Trail leads to a boardwalk and observation deck. The Live Oak Trail travels beneath stately trees draped with Spanish moss. Exploring this park is a joy you can experience many times over, especially with such a nice campground.

JONES LAKE
STATE PARK

HAVE YOU EVER HEARD of a bay lake? These natural lakes stretch from Florida to New Jersey, but are most prominent in the Carolinas. Bay lakes are usually oval in shape, pointed on a northwest to southeast axis, and are usually no deeper than ten feet. Theories about the origin of these lakes range from meteors crashing into the earth to gigantic prehistoric whales carving holes in ancient shallow seas with their tails. The term "bay" in bay lake refers to the preponderance of sweet bay and red bay trees growing around them. A bay lake, Jones Lake is the centerpiece of this quiet state park with a quality campground that is simply not used to the frequency it deserves.

The campground and recreation areas of Jones Lake State Park are situated on the southeastern shore of 224-acre Jones Lake. Cypress, bay, titi, and other moisture tolerant flora ring the lake. The campground is situated in slightly higher, more sandy terrain. Here, longleaf pine and turkey oaks predominate. These two trees are part of the longleaf-wiregrass ecosystem, which once covered over 20 million acres in the Southeast. This open woodland makes for a very attractive campground setting.

A paved road loops around the campground. The large sites have a floor of sand and pine needles. Pond pines and loblolly pines also grow among the longleaf pines. Turkey oaks, with their short limbs and scrubby appearance, stand beneath the pines. Young bay trees, sassafras, and cane shoot from the ground. The campsites have a mixture of sun and shade, but are more open than not. Normally, campsite privacy might be compromised, but the surprising lack of use at this attractive destination will likely leave you with no neighbors around.

Beyond campsite 7, a path leads from the campground to the Lake Trail and a fishing pier. The vegeta-

> *Pitch your tent among the longleaf pines by this Carolina bay lake.*

RATINGS

Beauty: ☆ ☆ ☆ ☆
Privacy: ☆ ☆ ☆
Spaciousness: ☆ ☆ ☆ ☆
Quiet: ☆ ☆ ☆ ☆
Security: ☆ ☆ ☆ ☆ ☆
Cleanliness: ☆ ☆ ☆ ☆

ADDRESS: Jones Lake State
Park
113 Jones Lake Drive
Elizabethtown, NC
28337

OPERATED BY: North Carolina State
Parks

INFORMATION: (910) 588-4550;
www.ncsparks.net

OPEN: March 15–
November 30

SITES: 20

EACH SITE HAS: Picnic table, fire
grate, trash can

ASSIGNMENT: First come, first
served; no reserva-
tions

REGISTRATION: Ranger will come by
and register you

FACILITIES: Hot showers, flush
toilets, water spigots

PARKING: At campsites only

FEE: $12 per night

ELEVATION: 75 feet

RESTRICTIONS: **Pets:** On leash only
Fires: In fire rings
only
Alcohol: Prohibited
Vehicles: None
Other: 14-day stay
limit in a 30-day
period

tion thickens as a wetland backs the campsites. Pass the access road to the group campground and reach sites that are more open, though most have enough shade to make it through a hot day.

A small bathhouse centers the loop. Summer and early fall will find younger families from nearby military bases pitching a tent. Campers can count on getting a site just about any weekend, except for summer holiday weekends. Even then, your chances of getting a site are pretty good.

A visitor center stands near Jones Lake and the center of activity. Interpretive ranger programs are held on weekends. A pretty picnic area dotted with scattered trees among lush grass overlooks the lake, and a dock leads out to a boathouse where canoes and paddleboats can be rented at very reasonable rates. The park swim beach is here, too, marked by buoys that extend far out into the dark waters.

If you want to hike, take the Lake Trail. It extends for 3 miles, encircling the scenic body of water. Short side trails lead to the lake's edge and good views. Beginning near the nature center, a shorter walk can be made on the Nature Trail, which makes a 1-mile loop.

A boat launch enables those with their own watercraft to access the lake. Motors of ten horsepower and below are allowed. Jones Lake is highly acidic and this limits the fishing. However, you can vie for yellow perch, pickerel, catfish, and small sunfish. A fishing pier extends into the lake from near the campground for those without boats. Nearby Salters Lake, also a Carolina bay lake within the park's 2,000 plus acres, is managed as a natural area. Visitors can access it after getting a permit from the ranger station. Carved from the surrounding Bladen Lakes State Forest, Jones Lake State Park is quiet and undeveloped, which, as a tent camper, you will enjoy.

MAP

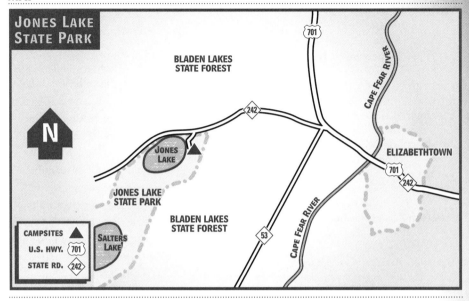

From Elizabethtown, follow NC 242 north for 4 miles to the state park, which will be on your left.

LUMBER RIVER
STATE PARK

> *All the sites on the wild and scenic Lumber River are walk-in tent sites.*

AS A FEDERALLY DESIGNATED Wild and Scenic River, the Lumber is officially special. The state of North Carolina recognized the Lumber River's beauty and is adding a serpentine state park along it, protecting wild stretches and developing other park units that allow access to riverside camping and water-access points with rest rooms and picnic areas. This Princess Ann Unit of the park has a walk-in tent campground, where you can enjoy the river and the land around it. Nearby outfitters allow even the boatless to float down the Lumber and return to this campground that seems to have tent campers in mind.

The campground is located in lush, dark, and cool woods near the Princess Ann access boat ramp. Seven campsites are grouped together and two campsites are located directly along the Lumber River. The main camping area is set in luxuriant woods on a sloping hill leading toward the Lumber River. Water oaks, sweetgums, and understory oaks dominate the forest. The smaller bay trees have to work hard to gain light from the thick overhead canopy. A paved path leads to disabled-access campsite 1. This site, like all the others, has been leveled using landscaping timbers. A gravel path continues to campsite 2. Campsite 3 is at the lower end of the hill, closer to the Lumber River. Campsite 4 has oaks with outstretched limbs shading it. Campsite 5 is closer to the river. Campsite 6 has the farthest walk, but even this is no more than 75 yards. This campsite is open in the center and has the most privacy from the sites around it. Campsite 7 is highest on the hill. It is very shady and has pine needles for a carpet. But the site is small and was added as an afterthought. A short trail leads to the final two campsites. Walk past the boat ramp and begin downstream along the beautiful Lumber River. Reach campsite 8 first, then campsite 9. Cypress trees draped in Spanish moss stand along the

RATINGS

Beauty: ✿ ✿ ✿ ✿
Privacy: ✿ ✿ ✿ ✿
Spaciousness: ✿ ✿ ✿
Quiet: ✿ ✿ ✿ ✿
Security: ✿ ✿ ✿ ✿ ✿
Cleanliness: ✿ ✿ ✿ ✿

river. A cypress/gum swamp lies on the other side of the campsites. This area is level and shady, exuding the beauty of the river.

Bald cypresses, with their knees protruding from the water, line the Lumber River and rich stands of cane overlook the tannin-stained, tea-colored water. A bluff that rises from this side of the river, attracted early settlers who formed the community of Princess Ann. The bluff served as a buffer against Lumber River floods. Now, the park headquarters, a picnic area, and a hiking trail extend along this bluff. A boat ramp is conveniently located beside the camping area. Here, canoeists and kayakers launch their craft for short trips in the immediate area or use it as a takeout, making shuttle runs upriver. This dark serpent of flowing watery wildness runs for 115 miles, making overnight wilderness trips viable. Eighty-one of the river miles are designated Wild and Scenic. If you don't have two cars for a shuttle, River Bend Outfitters is located near the park. Located in the town of Fair Bluff, they offer shuttle services and also rent canoes and kayaks. For more information call (910) 649-5998. Check the park office for a list of other outfitters operating along the Lumber River.

A hiking trail extends from the picnic area along the Lumber River, and heads upriver for a mile. Check out Griffin's Whorl, where the Lumber River reverses flow before resuming downriver. Along the way, the trail passes an observation deck/fishing pier. Folks angle here for crappie, sunfish, crappie, and largemouth bass. Bank fishing also takes places along the shore near the campground. Hopefully, you will take time to enjoy a tent camping adventure here on the Lumber River.

KEY INFORMATION

ADDRESS:	Lumber River State Park
	2819 Princess Ann Road
	Orrum, NC 28369
OPERATED BY:	North Carolina State Parks
INFORMATION:	(910) 628-9844; www.ncsparks.net
OPEN:	Year-round
SITES:	9
EACH SITE HAS:	Picnic tale, fire ring, lantern post, tent pad, trash can
ASSIGNMENT:	First come, first served; no reservations
REGISTRATION:	Ranger will come by and register you
FACILITIES:	Water spigot, vault toilet
PARKING:	At boat ramp parking area
FEE:	$8 per night
ELEVATION:	80 feet
RESTRICTIONS:	**Pets:** On leash only
	Fires: In fire rings only
	Alcohol: Prohibited
	Vehicles: None
	Other: 14-day stay limit in 30-day period

MAP

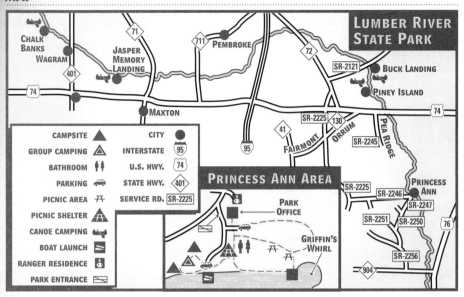

GETTING THERE

From Exit 14 on I-95, take US 74, Andrew Jackson Highway, east for 11.3 miles to Creek Road/State Road 2225. (There will be a sign for Orrum Middle School at this turn). Turn right onto Creek Road and follow it for 5.3 miles to Princess Ann Road. Turn left on Princess Ann Road and follow it for 2 miles to reach the Princess Ann Unit of Lumber River State Park, on your left.

MERCHANTS MILLPOND STATE PARK

MERCHANTS MILLPOND STATE PARK is simply one of North Carolina's finest tent camping destinations. This quiet getaway in the northeastern state is overlooked because it has neither the glamour of the ocean nor the lure of the mountains; nevertheless this coastal-plain park shines brightly. The actual Merchants Millpond is a "mini Okefenokee Swamp," offering a brooding, wetland ecosystem ideal for canoeing and fishing in the relaxing quiet that only nature can provide. The surrounding high ground has its appeal, too, with many hiking trails traveling the land. To top it off, the campground seems to have been designed for tent campers.

As with all park facilities here, the campground is appealing and well maintained. The campground is laid out in a classic loop with a mere 20 campsites. Overhead, loblolly pines tower above red and white oaks, maples, and thick understory brush such as myrtle oak. Pine needles carpet the forest floor, and shade is abundant. Elevated tent pads, filled with sand, allow for easy staking of your tent and quick drainage in case of rain. The campsites are located far from one another, which added with the thick woods, makes for maximum privacy. Most sites are on the outside of the loop, but here, every site is a winner, no matter where it is located. Small trails lead to the center of the loop where a modern bathhouse lies. Most sites can accommodate a large tent and screen shelter, if you so desire. Spring and fall are the best time to visit Merchants Millpond. Summer can be hot and buggy. Late March through April and mid-October are the busiest times, though campsites are available just about any weekend. Winter is quiet. Park gates are locked every evening until morning light, making for maximum camper safety. An emergency phone at the ranger station allows quick departure, as a park ranger lives on-site.

> *This is the unsung jewel of the North Carolina State Park system.*

RATINGS

Beauty: ☆ ☆ ☆ ☆ ☆
Privacy: ☆ ☆ ☆ ☆ ☆
Spaciousness: ☆ ☆ ☆ ☆
Quiet: ☆ ☆ ☆ ☆ ☆
Security: ☆ ☆ ☆ ☆ ☆
Cleanliness: ☆ ☆ ☆ ☆ ☆

ADDRESS: Merchants Millpond
State Park
71 US Highway 158E
Gatesville, NC 27938

OPERATED BY: North Carolina State
Parks

INFORMATION: (252) 357-1191;
www.ncsparks.net

OPEN: Year-round

SITES: 20

EACH SITE HAS: Picnic table, fire
ring, lantern post,
tent pad, waste can

ASSIGNMENT: First come, first
served; no reserva-
tions

REGISTRATION: Ranger will come by
and register you

FACILITIES: Hot showers, flush
toilets, water, and
showers on from
mid-March through
November

PARKING: At campsites only

FEE: $12 per night

ELEVATION: 25 feet

RESTRICTIONS: **Pets:** On leash only
Fires: In fire rings
only
Alcohol: Prohibited
Vehicles: Two per
site
Other: 14-day stay
limit in 30-day
period

Bennetts Creek was dammed over 180 years ago, forming Merchants Millpond. The elevated pond provided waterpower to operate a gristmill and later a sawmill in Gates County. The 760-acre pond, ringed with cypress and gum trees, is filled with fish and other wildlife. Lassiter Swamp occupies the upper reaches of Bennetts Creek and the millpond. Canoes are available for rent at very reasonable prices, to tour the swamp or for casting a line to catch bream, crappie, or largemouth bass. Only electric motors are allowed on the lake, making it a quiet retreat to nature. There are even backcountry canoe campsites for the adventurous. Check at the park office for canoe rental information.

The park can also be explored by land. Several foot trails course through the woods and along the wetlands. One trail even has a backpacker's campsite. If you hike no other path, at least check out the Cypress Point Trail. Cypress Point Trail makes a quarter-mile loop along the edge of the millpond, overlooking the swamp from a boardwalk. The Coleman Trail extends for 2 miles. It also offers good views of the millpond and travels through several habitats. This is a good birding trail, especially during spring and fall migrations. The Lassiter Trail is the master path of the park. You can pick it up directly from the campground via a 0.4-mile spur trail. Make the 5-mile loop by passing along the north side of the millpond and along Lassiter Swamp. A park fire road cuts the loop in half. Park programs are held on weekends and will help inform you about this special swath of the coastal plain, which plainly, you should not miss.

MAP

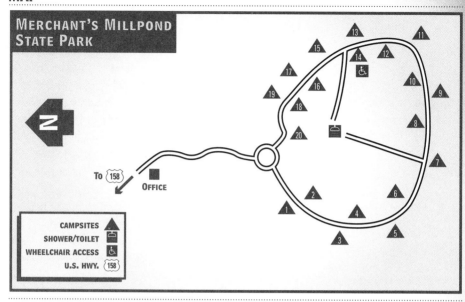

MERCHANT'S MILLPOND STATE PARK

N

CAMPSITES
SHOWER/TOILET
WHEELCHAIR ACCESS
U.S. HWY. 158

To 158
OFFICE

GETTING THERE

From Exit 173 on I-95, drive east on US 158 for 61 miles to the park, located on your right, west of Sunbury.

NEUSE RIVER CAMPGROUND

> *This national forest campground has received a face-lift and is set for more improvements.*

LOCALLY KNOWN AS Flanners Beach, this revamped bluffside campground on the lower Neuse River is a fine recreation destination. The well-kept camp received a face-lift after storm damage from a series of hurricanes in the late 1990s, most notably Hurricane Fran in 1996. A paved hiking/biking trail loops through the campground. Flanners Beach, a sandy shoreline along the tidally influenced lower Neuse River, has been a swimming and waterside recreation destination for a long time.

The campground is laid out in a loop. Passing the campground host, there for your security, tall loblolly pines reach for the sky, above an understory of smaller oaks and sweetgums. You will immediately notice that the campground has a landscaped look, as opposed to random tree growth. Starting in the year 2000, brushy live oaks, willows, and many other trees were planted, especially between campsites to add campsite privacy. Whether it returns to a completely natural look over time is irrelevant, because the vegetation adds to the attractiveness of Neuse River. More improvements are slated for the future, such as an additional loop just for tent campers. As it is, the first several campsites in the loop do have electricity, attracting the big rigs. But let not your heart be troubled, as 33 out of 42 sites do not have electricity. The sites on the inside of the loop have more shade and vegetation than those on the outside of the loop, but they are smaller as well. A trip or two around the loop will reveal a mixture of sunny/shady spots. Several campsites are close to the river, but the bluff prevents quick access to Flanners Beach. Sites are generally available on all but summer holiday weekends, and always during the week. A modern bathhouse centers the loop, and is easily accessed by all campers.

RATINGS

Beauty: ✿ ✿ ✿
Privacy: ✿ ✿ ✿
Spaciousness: ✿ ✿ ✿ ✿
Quiet: ✿ ✿ ✿
Security: ✿ ✿ ✿ ✿
Cleanliness: ✿ ✿ ✿

The area encompassing the Croatan National Forest has a long history. Its name was likely derived from the Croatan Indians, who settled in villages along the Neuse River. The nearby town of New Bern, North Carolina's second oldest, was established in 1710. Timber from the area became important in the production of tar. Later, small farms were established, but were bought out, along with larger holdings, to establish the Croatan National Forest in 1936, for timber management and watershed protection. Recreation areas were developed over the decades, including Neuse River Campground. Always known as Flanners Beach, an errant mapmaker decided to name the campground after the nearby Neuse River. The name has never caught on, and locals call the area Flanners Beach to this day.

A paved recreation trail is open to bikes and hikers. It winds through the thick woods of the Neuse River bluff, about 30 feet above the Neuse River, and a tupelo swamp. A paved trail also connects the campground to an appealing picnic area, where towering pines and hardwoods shade a grassy lawn. Wooden steps lead down to Flanners Beach. The tan sand, littered with driftwood, extends for several yards in each direction, making for ample sunning and relaxing room. I enjoyed relaxing and looking over the water here. No alcoholic beverages are allowed at the swim beach and picnic area.

The Neuse River at this point is more of a bay than an inland river. Anglers can cast a line for striped bass, sunfish, largemouth bass, flounder, and crappie. The nearest boat ramp in the Croatan is at Cahooque Creek. Croatan National Forest offers other recreation opportunities on the tidal estuaries and freshwater lakes. Hikers can tackle the 26-mile Neusiok Trail, which crosses the 161,000-acre national forest. On the way in to Neuse River, stop at the ranger station for more information. Supplies can be had back in New Bern.

ADDRESS: Neuse River Campground 114 East Fisher Ave. New Bern, NC 28560

OPERATED BY: U.S. Forest Service

INFORMATION: (252) 638-5628; www.cs.unca.edu/nfsnc

OPEN: Year-round

SITES: 44

EACH SITE HAS: Picnic table, fire grate, lantern post, some have electricity

ASSIGNMENT: First come, first served; no reservations

REGISTRATION: Self-registration on site

FACILITIES: Hot showers, water spigots, flush toilets

PARKING: At campsites only

FEE: $12 per night, $17 per night electric sites

ELEVATION: 30 feet

RESTRICTIONS: Pets: On leash only
Fires: In fire rings only
Alcohol: At campsites only
Vehicles: None
Other: 14-day stay limit

MAP

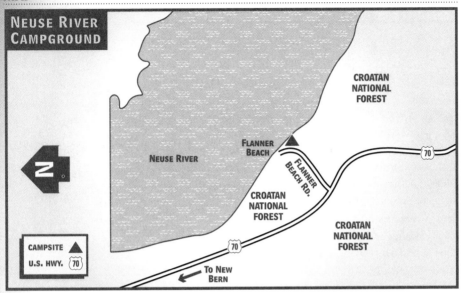

NEUSE RIVER CAMPGROUND

CROATAN NATIONAL FOREST

CROATAN NATIONAL FOREST

CROATAN NATIONAL FOREST

NEUSE RIVER

FLANNER BEACH

FLANNER BEACH RD.

70

70

CAMPSITE ▲

U.S. HWY. 70

To New Bern

GETTING THERE

From New Bern, drive 12 miles east on US 70 to Flanners Beach Road, 2 miles beyond the Croatan Rangers Station, on your left. Turn left on Flanners Beach Road and follow it for 1.5 miles to reach the campground.

OCRACOKE ISLAND CAMPGROUND

O CRACOKE ISLAND IS ACCESSIBLE only by ferry, but the extra effort reaps scenic rewards. Most of the island is part of the Cape Hatteras National Seashore, and is kept in its natural state. The village of Ocracoke is a worthy destination itself. It harks back to a 1950s fishing village, with its cottages, narrow streets, and lack of franchise operations. The natural setting, the village, and the campground combine to make a relaxing getaway worth a few days or more of your life.

The campground itself is the least inviting thing on the island, but it will suffice as your headquarters for exploring Ocracoke. The 137 campsites are located in a flat behind dunes that separate you from the beach and the Atlantic Ocean. Most of the campsites are on the main loop, which is broken by three crossroads. Some small cedar and other trees, pruned back by the relentless wind, dot the otherwise grassy campground. The loop curves around to reach the so-called "dune sites." These campsites are larger and are a short walk toward the beach from the paved parking pad. Other sites have average tent areas directly by the parking pad. Even the dune sites are open to the sun. The sites on the inside of the loop are small and pinched-in together.

The loop curves away from the beach, but even these sites are an easy walk to the beach. These sites, located away from the water, back up to a wetland, which can be problematic if the mosquitoes are biting. The campsites on the loop crossroads are mostly flat, grassy, and open to the sun. Three separate bathroom areas with cold showers are spread throughout the campground.

Reservations can be made in advance. After making a reservation, you are guaranteed a campsite, but you cannot pick out a specific site. A timely arrival is recommended even with a reservation, especially on

> *This island campground is accessible only by car ferry.*

RATINGS

Beauty: ✿ ✿ ✿
Privacy: ✿
Spaciousness: ✿ ✿
Quiet: ✿ ✿ ✿ ✿ ✿
Security: ✿ ✿ ✿ ✿
Cleanliness: ✿ ✿ ✿

ADDRESS: Ocracoke Island
Campground
Route 1, Box 675
Manteo, NC 27954

OPERATED BY: National Park
Service

INFORMATION: (252) 473-2111,
www.nps.gov/caha;
reservation, (800)
365-CAMP; ferry
information, (800)
293-3779 or at
www.ncferry.org

OPEN: Friday of Easter
weekend through
mid-October

SITES: 136

EACH SITE HAS: Picnic table, upright
grill

ASSIGNMENT: First come, first
served and by reser-
vation

REGISTRATION: At campground
entrance booth

FACILITIES: Cold showers, water
spigots, flush toilets

PARKING: At campsites only

FEE: $18 per night

ELEVATION: 20 feet

RESTRICTIONS: **Pets:** On leash only
Fires: In upright
grills only
Alcohol: At camp-
sites only
Vehicles: Must be
parked on paved
surface only

weekends. Reservations can be made only between mid-May and mid-September. Reservations are highly recommended on holiday weekends and from early July through mid-August. Be aware that mosquitoes can be a problem after wet spells, and mosquito repellent and a screen shelter will make your stay much more enjoyable. Furthermore, if you are taking either the Cedar Island ferry or the Swan Quarter ferry, it's also wise to make reservations for your arrival and departure, especially during the busy season. I recommend coming during the shoulder seasons, when the crowds are gone, the village of Ocracoke is in really low gear, and the better campsites are available.

Life slows here on Ocracoke Island. You can sense it as you walk the beach. A great place for quiet beachcombing is the beach access area across from the pony pens. More about the pony pens later. No cars are allowed on the beach here and no development can be seen. Cars are allowed on the beach near the campground. Sea kayaking is popular on the Pamlico Sound side of the island, and boats of all sorts can be rented in the village of Ocracoke. You can also rent bikes for pedaling around the village, charter a sportfishing boat, or eat in a unique restaurant (no franchises allowed!), visit the Ocracoke Lighthouse, built in the early 1800s, or just sit back on a bench at Silver Lake Harbor and watch the boats come and go. Take the Ocracoke Historical Interpretive Trail to learn about the lengthy past of this land. This place really does have character. Supplies can be had in the village.

The ponies that once roamed Ocracoke are now taken care of by the park service. They are quartered a few miles from the campground. The animals are thought to have swum ashore from a Spanish shipwreck long ago. An interpretive trail travels near the horse pens. Another interpretive trail, the Hardwood Hammocks Trail, travels into the island interior. The path starts just across the road from the campground. Start your planning now, for a trip to Ocracoke Island.

MAP

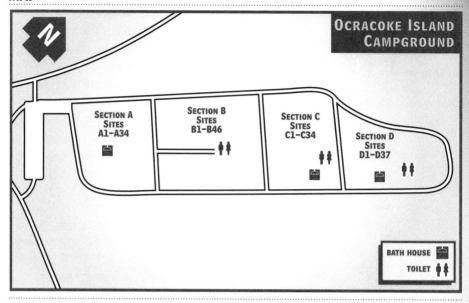

OCRACOKE ISLAND CAMPGROUND

SECTION A
SITES
A1–A34

SECTION B
SITES
B1–B46

SECTION C
SITES
C1–C34

SECTION D
SITES
D1–D37

BATH HOUSE
TOILET

GETTING THERE

From the intersection of US 64/264 and US 158 just south of Nags Head, drive south on NC 12 for 59 miles to the ferry at the southwest end of Hatteras Island. From here, take the free ferry over to Ocracoke Island. Once off the ferry, keep south on NC 12 for 9.5 miles to reach the campground, on your left. There are two other, longer toll ferry options to reach Ocracoke Island. For more ferry information call (800) 293-3779.

SOUTH CAROLINA **UPCOUNTRY**

BURRELLS FORD CAMPGROUND

BEFORE THE **C**HATTOOGA **WAS** declared a Wild and Scenic River, campers could drive all the way to Burrells Ford Campground. Since then, a protective corridor has been established, effectively cutting off all direct auto access to the campground. This has had mixed results: it has limited the use of the campground but has cut maintenance as well. The short walk may deter some tent campers, but you can be guaranteed no RVs will ever be at Burrells Ford!

Follow the old jeep road down to the river, entering the protected corridor. The road forks at the river bottom. The bottom is forested in tall white pines, with a thick understory of holly trees, rhododendron, and mountain laurel. The Chattooga runs shallow and clear directly in front of the campground, no doubt the ford of days gone by. On the other side of the river lies the state of Georgia, deeply shaded in thick, jungle-like vegetation. Deep pools lie both up- and downstream of the campground, beckoning the camper to drop a line or take a dip. Rainbow and brown trout thrive in the mountain water.

The right fork of the old jeep road leads directly to the Chattooga. Campsites are spread along both sides of the road. Most sites are cooled beneath the shady canopy, but some lie in a glade that receives enough sun for grass to grow. All the sites offer maximum privacy, as they are well away from one another. You won't be able to carry enough stuff from your automobile to the campground to utilize all the space offered at each campsite. Although, on my visit, one enterprising fellow toted his belongings down from the parking area in a wheelbarrow.

The left fork road enters the south side of the river bottom after crossing the clear and cool Kings Creek. Here you'll find more primitive sites: usually just a flat spot, a fire ring, and an occasional picnic table or

> *The Chattooga River and Ellicott Rock Wilderness are just a few footsteps away from this primitive campground.*

RATINGS

Beauty: ✪ ✪ ✪ ✪
Privacy: ✪ ✪ ✪ ✪ ✪
Spaciousness: ✪ ✪ ✪ ✪ ✪
Quiet: ✪ ✪ ✪ ✪ ✪
Security: ✪ ✪ ✪
Cleanliness: ✪ ✪ ✪

KEY INFORMATION

ADDRESS: Burrells Ford Campground 112 Andrew Pickens Circle Mountain Rest, SC 2964

OPERATED BY: U.S. Forest Service

INFORMATION: (864) 638-9568; www.fs.fed.us/r8/fms

OPEN: Year-round

SITES: Sites are not designated, but there is room for 9 tents

EACH SITE HAS: Picnic table, fire ring, lantern post

ASSIGNMENT: First come, first served; no reservations

REGISTRATION: Not necessary

FACILITIES: Hand-pumped water, pit toilet

PARKING: At Burrells Ford parking area

FEE: None

ELEVATION: 2,000 feet

RESTRICTIONS: Pets: On leash only
Fires: In fire rings only
Alcohol: At campsites only
Vehicles: In parking area only, no RVs or trailers
Other: Pack it in, pack it out; must carry tents one-third of a mile to site

lantern post. In a nearby flat, just upstream on Kings Creek, a very isolated site backs up against a steep hill for the tent camper seeking the ultimate in privacy. The left fork road intersects the Foothills Trail along the river; there you'll encounter many secluded and flat campsites. Solitude is yours, to say the least.

This place is rustic and, as would be expected, amenities are minimal at Burrells Ford. Your arms will get a workout at the hand-pump well near the head of the campground. A pair of pit toilets are available for your basic comfort.. After all, it is within a wild and scenic river corridor and borders the Ellicott Rock Wilderness.

If you would like to see more of the attractive riverine ecosystem of the Chattooga, you only need to choose whether to go up or down the river. Down the Chattooga is the Foothills Trail. It winds along the river past Big Bend Falls for some 5 miles to Licklog Creek before turning southeast toward Oconee State Park. You can keep south along the river for 4.8 miles on the Chattooga Trail to Ridley Fields and SC 28. But first, tune up with a short 0.3-mile hike up Kings Creek to a woodsy waterfall, then return to camp.

Upstream and north from Burrells Ford, the Foothills Trail climbs away from the river along Medlin Mountain on its journey to Table Rock State Park nearly 70 miles away. If you stay north along the river, you'll soon enter the 7,000-acre Ellicott Rock Wilderness on the north section of the Chattooga Trail. It leads 4 scenic miles past riverside beaches to Ellicott Rock. This spot was selected in 1811 by a surveyor named Ellicott to designate the exact location where the Carolinas and Georgia came together. Surveyor Andrew Ellicott chiseled "NC" in 1811 on this trailside marker. The actual point where the three states meet is Commissioner's Rock, a few feet distant. This rock, extending into the Chatooga River, is the true boundary. Stand here and you can be in three states at once. Take the short side trail to Spoon Auger Falls on your way back.

It takes a little effort to reach Burrells Ford Campground, but you will be well rewarded. The Chattooga deserves its Wild and Scenic status, and the surrounding mountain lands are wild and scenic as well.

MAP

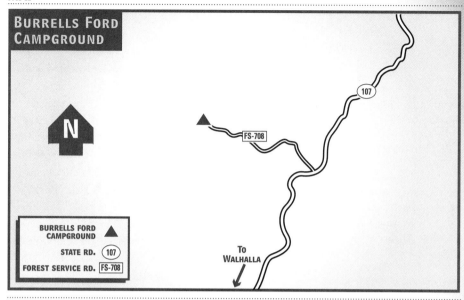

BURRELLS FORD
CAMPGROUND

107

FS-708

To
WALHALLA

BURRELLS FORD
CAMPGROUND ▲

STATE RD. 107

FOREST SERVICE RD. FS-708

GETTING THERE

From Walhalla drive north
on SC 28 for 8.5 miles to
SC 107, then turn right. Follow SC 107 for 8.9 miles.
Then turn left on gravel FS
708. Descend on FS 708 for
3 miles. Burrells Ford parking area will be on your left.

CHERRY HILL CAMPGROUND

> *Cherry Hill is South Carolina's finest upcountry campground.*

CHERRY HILL CAMPGROUND is the focal point for the Cherry Hill Recreation Area. And, as one of the best national forest campgrounds in the Southern Appalachians, it is a fine place to be. The campground, located in the shallow upper valley of West Fork Creek, lies covered with an abundant understory beneath a towering forest of hardwood and pine. The Forest Service must work hard to keep the vegetation from reclaiming this land.

Just off SC 107 is the entrance to Cherry Hill Campground. Immediately to the left is a circular turnaround, known as the overflow area. It once was home to a settler, whose chimney is still standing just off the loop; a short path leads to the ruins. Four new campsites have been carved into the woods there, but you must park your car on the loop and carry your belongings a few feet from the loop to the new campsites.

The main campground lies beyond the overflow area on a short spur road that descends to tranquil West Fork Creek. Just past the self-service pay station are two isolated sites on their own mini-loop. A water spigot is nearby. Three other sites are located off the spur road before you reach the main loop, which makes a large oval beside the West Fork.

All the sites along the West Fork are shrouded in rhododendron and are ideal for campers who like deep, lush woods. Four relatively open sites are located on the inside of the main loop and offer a generous amount of space for even the most gear-laden camper. The sites away from the West Fork back against a hill beneath more open woods. Three water spigots are situated throughout the main loop. A clean, well-kept comfort station is at the north end of the loop; it has warm showers and flush toilets. There are no electric hook-ups.

RATINGS

Beauty: ✿ ✿ ✿ ✿ ✿
Privacy: ✿ ✿ ✿ ✿
Spaciousness: ✿ ✿ ✿ ✿ ✿
Quiet: ✿ ✿ ✿ ✿
Security: ✿ ✿ ✿ ✿
Cleanliness: ✿ ✿ ✿ ✿ ✿

Near the comfort station, a small circular drive splits off the main loop. It holds four campsites with large parking areas, apparently designed for RVers, who were the only campers I saw at that spot during my visit. The circle has its own water spigot.

A campground host is stationed at Cherry Hill and keeps the place immaculate and safe. This only adds to the relaxing atmosphere of the area. Just as you get really comfortable, a notion will strike you to venture beyond your folding chair to explore more of the beauty of Sumter National Forest. And you don't even have to leave Cherry Hill to walk some of the area trails. For starters, try the Cherry Hill Nature Trail. It leaves the campground and makes a half-mile loop among the ferns and brush of the white pine forest.

The Winding Stairs Trail also leaves from the campground. Follow it down as it switchbacks through an oak forest along the south side of the West Fork. I can only guess that the gentle switchbacking led to the Winding Stairs name. At any rate, after a mile, you'll come to a small but steep waterfall, as West Fork Creek has picked up some volume on its way to merge with Crane Creek. After the fall, the Winding Stairs Trail veers south to Crane Creek, then returns to West Fork only to end at 3.5 miles on Forest Service Road 710.

If you want bigger water, the Chattooga Wild and Scenic River is only a stroll away on the Big Bend Trail. The trail starts just across SC 107 from the campground and leads 2.7 miles west into the protected corridor of the Chattooga just above Big Bend Falls. From there, trails lead along the river in both directions for miles. Either way you go, you'll soon understand why this border river between South Carolina and Georgia is protected. The flora, fauna, and tumbling white water are yours to appreciate. And the fishing's good too.

Cherry Hill is a quality campground in an attractive forest setting. And for ten bucks, it is a superlative value. Get all your supplies back in Walhalla, because once you're at Cherry Hill, you won't want to spoil your vacation with an early return to civilization.

ADDRESS: Cherry Hill Campground 112 Andrew Pickens Circle Mountain Rest, SC 2964

OPERATED BY: U.S. Forest Service

INFORMATION: (864) 638-9568; www.fs.fed.us/r8/fms

OPEN: May–September

SITES: 29

EACH SITE HAS: Picnic table, fire pit, lantern post

ASSIGNMENT: First come, first served; no reservations

REGISTRATION: Self-registration on site

FACILITIES: Water, flush toilets, hot showers

PARKING: At campsites only

FEE: $10 per night

ELEVATION: 2,250 feet

RESTRICTIONS: **Pets:** On leash only
Fires: In fire pits only
Alcohol: At campsites only
Vehicles: None
Other: 6 people per campsite; tents in designated areas only

MAP

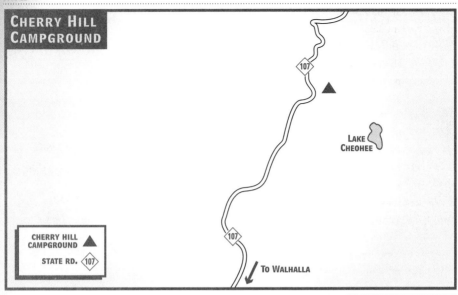

CHERRY HILL CAMPGROUND

107

LAKE CHEOHEE

CHERRY HILL CAMPGROUND ▲

STATE RD. 107

107

To WALHALLA

GETTING THERE

From Walhalla drive north on SC 28 for 8.5 miles to SC 107, then turn right. Follow SC 107 for 7.5 miles. The entrance to Cherry Hill Campground will be on your right.

DEVILS FORK
STATE PARK

HAVE YOU EVER SEEN Lake Jocassee? Others may disagree, but I believe this impoundment to be South Carolina's most beautiful lake. A richly forested shoreline overlooks emerald water against a backdrop of the Blue Ridge Mountains. On the lake's northern shores are the Jocassee Gorges, steep valleys where waterfalls are fed by cool clear streams. Devils Fork State Park occupies some of Lake Jocassee's awesome shoreline, where walk-in tent sites abut the shoreline and offer instant water access.

Being a water-oriented park, it comes as no surprise that the campground is near the shoreline, but, even better, the walk-in tent sites are close to the lake. The main tent camping area spurs onto a wooded peninsula extending into the lake, with a paved trail leading down to the campsites. Descend along a rib ridge covered in mountain laurel, oaks, pines, and tulip trees. Campsites T-1 through T-8 dip toward the lake but are closer to the parking area. The mountain slope has been leveled at each site. Campsites T-9 through T-15 overlook the water and offer a view of the mountains beyond the lake. Landscaping timbers have been installed at the campsites and beyond to slow erosion. Campsites T-16 through T-19 are too close to one another but overlook the lake; T-18 is the best of this bunch. Campsite T-20 is closest to the walk-in parking area. The least appealing sites here are T-6, T-8, and T-19, but they are still better than most campsites at other campgrounds. A water spigot lies at the beginning of the walk-in camper access trail.

A second set of walk-in tent sites is accessible from the day-use area, near a playground. Take a short gravel path to reach sites T-21 through T-25, where the woods are more open. Campsite T-22 is very near the lake. Campsites T-23 and T-24 are a little too close together. Campsite T-25 has the farthest walk, but ends

> *Enjoy the walk-in sites that overlook South Carolina's most beautiful lake.*

RATINGS

Beauty: ✩ ✩ ✩ ✩
Privacy: ✩ ✩ ✩
Spaciousness: ✩ ✩ ✩
Quiet: ✩ ✩ ✩
Security: ✩ ✩ ✩ ✩ ✩
Cleanliness: ✩ ✩ ✩ ✩

ADDRESS: Devils Fork State Park
161 Holcombe Circle
Salem, SC 29676

OPERATED BY: South Carolina State Parks

INFORMATION: (864) 944-2639; www.southcarolina parks.com

OPEN: Year-round

SITES: 25 walk-in tent sites, 59 other

EACH SITE HAS: Walk-in tent sites have picnic table, fire ring, tent pad; other sites also have water and electricity

ASSIGNMENT: First come, first serve and by reservation

REGISTRATION: At park office

FACILITIES: Hot showers, flush toilets, water spigots, laundry

PARKING: At walk-in parking area and at campsites

FEE: Walk-in tent sites $9 per night, others $18 per night

ELEVATION: 1,150 feet

RESTRICTIONS: **Pets:** On leash only
Fires: In fire rings only
Alcohol: Prohibited
Vehicles: Two per campsite
Other: 6 persons per walk-in campsite

up near some of the drive-up sites in the main campground area. A water spigot is near these sites.

The main drive-up campground has two loops. Tent pads are at most sites. Trees shade the sites and ample vegetation screens the sites from one another. Any of these sites will suffice, but the tent sites are far more desirable. And since all sites are reservable, why not go for the ones you like? Reservations are strongly recommended, as the campground will fill nearly every weekend from Easter through fall.

The acreage of this park is fairly small but there are two hiking trails. The 1.5-mile Oconee Bells Nature Trail takes you by places where the rare Oconee Bell wildflower grows. The Bear Cove Trail makes a 3.5-mile loop and starts at the day-use area. Most recreation centers on this superlatively beautiful lake. You'll see campers swimming near their sites, as no supervised swim area exists. Watercraft access to the lake is made easy at the park boat ramp. If you don't have a boat or want to get shuttled across the lake to explore some of the Jocassee Gorges, Hoyett's Bait and Tackle is just outside the park. They have fishing gear and bait, rent boats, offer shuttles, and guided sightseeing and fishing tours on Lake Jocassee. Call them at (864) 944-9016.

Jocassee Lake is worth seeing. You can check out all the rivers that feed Lake Jocassee from gorges coming out of the mountains—Whitewater River, Devils Fork Creek, Horsepasture River, and Toxaway River. I have explored them via the Foothills Trail that runs along the north shore of Lake Jocassee and proclaim them a prize resource of both North and South Carolina. Make a reservation to tent camp at Devils Fork and explore Lake Jocassee, then see if you think it is South Carolina's most beautiful lake.

MAP

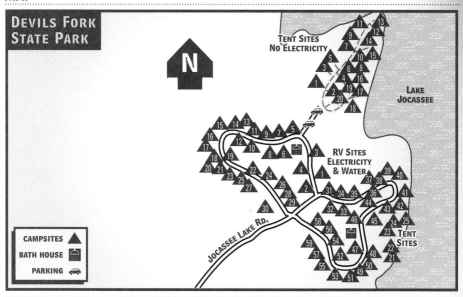

GETTING THERE

From Pickens, drive on US 178 north for 9 miles to SC 11. Turn left on SC 11 and follow it 12.5 miles to reach Jocassee Lake Road. Turn right on Jocassee Lake Road and follow it 3.5 miles to reach the park.

JONES GAP
STATE PARK

South Carolina operates this ecological treasure more sensitively than most other state parks.

THIS STATE PARK and the adjacent Caesars Head State Park are operated as low-impact wilderness parks. This means they are not designed like traditional parks with big drive-up campgrounds, parking lots, and heavy usage areas. Rather, the park facilities are integrated into an exceptional mountain landscape, leaving the emphasis on the natural, where foot trails lead along crystalline streams crashing over mossy boulders beneath cathedral-like forests, where rock faces offer sweeping vistas, and where spring wildflowers peek through leaves that colored the landscape the previous fall.

For tent campers "low impact" also means carrying your stuff to rustic walk-in tent campsites, and treading lightly on the land. It means packing your trash not only from your campsite but also from the entire park. It also means giving in to the spell the park lays on you, so that no matter what time of year you visit, it will make you want to return for more hiking through the Mountain Bridge Wilderness and taking in the sights.

Jones Gap State Park actually offers 29 campsites. The nine described below are within a half-mile of the camper parking area and are walk-in campsites. The other 22 sites are considered backcountry campsites. To reach the walk-in sites, leave the camper parking area and cross a bridge over the Middle Saluda River, deservedly South Carolina's first state scenic river. Ahead is the impressive log cabin that houses the park office and environmental learning center. This is where you register. If no one is there, use the nearby pay phone and call the pager number listed on the park office door. A ranger will come and assist you.

Now to the campsites, which are marked with green plastic posts. Campsites 1 through 4 are located past the old hatchery pool on the Hospital Rock Trail, to

RATINGS

Beauty: ✩ ✩ ✩ ✩ ✩
Privacy: ✩ ✩ ✩ ✩
Spaciousness: ✩ ✩ ✩
Quiet: ✩ ✩ ✩ ✩ ✩
Security: ✩ ✩ ✩ ✩ ✩
Cleanliness: ✩ ✩ ✩ ✩

your right as you face the log cabin. The paved trail leads to a dirt trail and the woods. Campsite 1 is along a small streamlet among boulders in dark rhododendron. Campsite 2 is a little on the sloped side, and is shaded by oaks. Campsite 3 is away from water in a notch between two ridge lines. Hickories and oaks shade the camp. Campsite 4 is near the pipeline feeding the fish hatchery pool and overlooks a mountain ravine.

Campsites 5 through 7 are actually closest to the camper parking area. These lead into woods from a path just to the left of the log cabin, with the Middle Saluda nearby. Campsite 5 is up a hill on a neat, rocky flat. The numerous embedded boulders there act as camp furniture. Campsite 6 is located in a flat directly beside the Middle Saluda. Campsite 7 is at the end of this short trail, less than 100 yards from the log cabin office. It is banked against a hillside, shaded by rhododendron near the river.

Campsites 8 and 9 are up the Jones Gap Trail heading directly up the Middle Saluda River from the camper parking area. Campsite 8 is large and surrounded by hardwoods. The noise of the river crashing over boulders will sing you to sleep. Campsite 9 is the hardest to reach, 0.4 miles from the parking area. It is large, too, and is also along the river. Rocks and sand form the campsite floor.

The campsites fill on the first nice weekends in spring, then taper off when the heat rises. Then, from mid-August until the leaves fall the campsites can fill any weekend. During the week, you can get a campsite anytime. The bath house, with a water spigot outside, is located near the log cabin. Be aware that the showers are open only from 6 p.m. to 8 a.m.

The picnic/log cabin/former hatchery area exudes tranquility. The mown grass contrasts with the verdant forests, the steep mountains and the crashing Middle Saluda River. You will wish you had a scenically located log cabin of your own. But visiting Jones Gap State Park is about hiking and exploring the Mountain Bridge Wilderness. Trails galore wind through the campground. One of my fondest outdoor memories occurred at Jones Gap State Park. I hiked the entire

ADDRESS: Jones Gap State Park 303 Jones Gap Road Marietta, SC 29661

OPERATED BY: South Carolina State Parks

INFORMATION: (864) 836-3647, www.southcarolina parks.com

OPEN: Year-round

SITES: 9 walk-in sites

EACH SITE HAS: Fire grate

ASSIGNMENT: First come, first served; no reservations

REGISTRATION: At log cabin ranger station

FACILITIES: Hot showers, flush toilets, water spigot

PARKING: At walk-in camper parking area

FEE: $3 per night

ELEVATION: 1,500 feet

RESTRICTIONS: **Pets:** On leash only **Fires:** In fire rings only **Alcohol:** Prohibited **Vehicles:** Two per campsite **Other:** Pack it in, pack it out

MAP

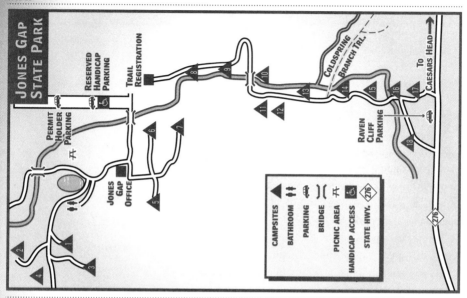

GETTING THERE

From Pickens, take SC 8 north for 15 miles to SC 11. Veer right onto SC 11 and follow it 2 miles to US 276. Turn right on US 276 and follow it 4 miles to River Falls Road. Turn left on River Falls Road and keep forward for 5.5 miles as it turns into Jones Gap Road to dead end at Jones Gap State Park.

Foothills Trail from Oconee State Park 90 miles to Jones Gap State Park in fall. The final morning dawned cool and crisp as wood smoke curled from my fire. I walked down through The Winds (as in wind a clock), along the numerous cascades of the Middle Saluda River. Framed in autumn color, I enjoyed the satisfaction of completing the entire trail with such an inspiring ending.

Jones Gap has many other trails and destinations in addition to the Middle Saluda. The combined area of Jones Gap and adjacent Caesars Head state parks is known as the Mountain Bridge Wilderness Area. A wilderness trail map, available at the park office, reveals much more than a weekend's worth of possibilities. Head to Raven Cliff Falls, or Hospital Rock, or hike up Coldspring Branch to enjoy wildflowers. A shorter loop includes the Rim of the Gap Trail and returns via Little Pinnacle Mountain on the Pinnacle Pass Trail. Jones Gap is all about trails and wilderness; just remember to leave the land in this mountain treasure as you found it.

KEOWEE-TOXAWAY STATE PARK

THIS AREA OF **SOUTH CAROLINA** is aptly named the Cherokee Foothills. The Cherokee thrived here long before white settlers ever laid eyes on this land. South Carolina recognizes this, and Keowee-Toxaway celebrates native culture in the natural setting of the Cherokee Foothills at this quiet, well-maintained state park.

Tent campers can enjoy the area by day and return to a great campground at night. It is situated on a well-wooded knoll that tastefully integrates the campsites with the steep terrain using well-placed landscaping timbers. Shade is abundant beneath the canopy of hickories and oaks, though a relatively light understory somewhat diminishes privacy.

Tent campers have their own separate loop. No loud generators humming in the background will interfere with your listening to the birds chirp. The 14 tent sites are all spacious and level enough to set up a normal amount of gear, but expect some seriously sloping topography if you stray from your designated area. That slope, though, allows for balcony-like views into the hollows beyond the campground knoll. The campsites on the interior of the loop are less steep beyond their timbered camping area. The tent pads at this state park are among the finest I have seen. They are slightly crowned in the center, allowing for quick runoff during those heavy mountain thunderstorms. It is just one more obvious sign that the campground is well designed.

Another plus is that you'll never have to go far for water. Three spigots are evenly distributed along the small loop. RVers and tenters share a comfort station located between the two separate loops. Hot showers and flush toilets are provided. Additional features include firewood for sale at the park office and excellent campground safety. This might be the safest camp-

> *Cherokee heritage, scenic hill country, mountain lakes, and a peaceful campground make Keowee-Toxaway an outstanding state park.*

RATINGS

Beauty: ✫ ✫ ✫ ✫
Privacy: ✫ ✫ ✫ ✫
Spaciousness: ✫ ✫ ✫ ✫
Quiet: ✫ ✫ ✫ ✫
Security: ✫ ✫ ✫ ✫ ✫
Cleanliness: ✫ ✫ ✫ ✫ ✫

ADDRESS:	Keowee-Toxaway State Park 108 Residence Drive Sunset, SC 29685
OPERATED BY:	South Carolina State Parks
INFORMATION:	(864) 868-2605; www.southcarolina parks.com
OPEN:	Year-round
SITES:	14 tents-only sites, 10 RV sites
EACH SITE HAS:	Tent pad, picnic table, fire ring with attached grill
ASSIGNMENT:	First come, first served; no reservations
REGISTRATION:	Ranger comes by to register guests
FACILITIES:	Water, flush toilets, hot showers
PARKING:	At campsites only
FEE:	$6.60 per night; RV sites, $11
ELEVATION:	1,000 feet
RESTRICTIONS:	**Pets:** On leash only **Fires:** In fire rings only **Alcohol:** Not allowed **Vehicles:** None **Other:** 14-day stay limit on one campsite

ground in the state. Park gates are locked at night and the ranger residence is just a stone's throw away from the tenters' loop.

Near the park office is the Cherokee Interpretive Center, which is the park's centerpiece that recognizes the area's Cherokee heritage. During my visit I learned quite a bit about Cherokee life before, during, and after the arrival of European settlers. The center also tells of the flora and fauna that inhabit the state park. Visit the Interpretive Center first and you'll have an enhanced appreciation of the historic and natural life of Keowee-Toxaway.

Just outside the Interpretive Center is the quarter-mile Cherokee Interpretive Trail. It winds through the woods and chronicles the evolution of the Cherokee tribe at four informative kiosks, culminating with the story of their removal from their ancestral lands along the infamous "Trail of Tears."

Other, longer trails carpet the park. The 4-mile Raven Rock Trail undulates amid the piney hills and hardwood hollows along clear creeks to a rock cliff overlooking Lake Keowee, then loops back via the Natural Bridge Trail to the park's Meeting House. A rock bridge spans Poe Creek along the Natural Bridge Trail. The 0.7-mile Lake Trail leads from the campground down to the shore of Lake Keowee. This park may be only 1,000 acres, but South Carolinians make the most of the scenic beauty packed into the small package.

Lake lovers have two nearby bodies of water to enjoy. Both Lake Keowee and Lake Jocassee are clean waters backed against the Blue Ridge with mountainous shorelines. Lake Keowee is the larger of the two lakes. It is a warm-water fishery, with bass and bream as its primary sportfish. Anglers will be surprised to find trout in Lake Jocassee's deep, cool waters. Nearby Devils Fork State Park is on Lake Jocassee and offers quality camping as well, with a special section of walk-in tent sites.

Overall, you will find understated Keowee-Toxaway State Park a pleasant surprise. The campground is ideal for tent campers who want an intimate, well-kept campground with plenty of amenities. The

MAP

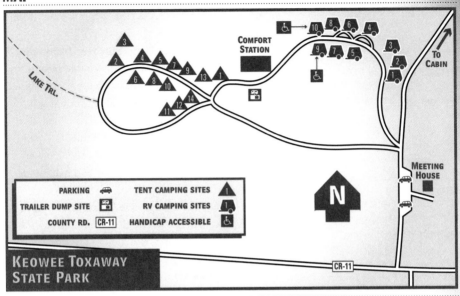

PARKING 🚗
TRAILER DUMP SITE ▦
COUNTY RD. CR-11

TENT CAMPING SITES ▲
RV CAMPING SITES 🚐
HANDICAP ACCESSIBLE ♿

KEOWEE TOXAWAY STATE PARK

CR-11

blending of Cherokee heritage and natural beauty was a master stroke by South Carolina park officials. Don't make the mistake of overlooking this small jewel of the Palmetto State.

GETTING THERE

From Pickens drive north on US 178 for 9 miles to SC 11. Turn left on SC 11 and drive for 7.9 miles to Keowee-Toxaway State Park.

OCONEE
STATE PARK

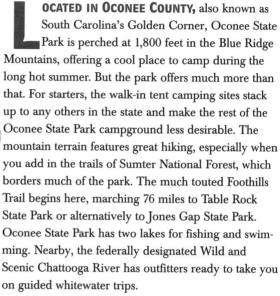

> *Oconee State Park is one example of the fine recreation destinations in South Carolina's Golden Corner.*

LOCATED IN **O**CONEE **C**OUNTY, also known as South Carolina's Golden Corner, Oconee State Park is perched at 1,800 feet in the Blue Ridge Mountains, offering a cool place to camp during the long hot summer. But the park offers much more than that. For starters, the walk-in tent camping sites stack up to any others in the state and make the rest of the Oconee State Park campground less desirable. The mountain terrain features great hiking, especially when you add in the trails of Sumter National Forest, which borders much of the park. The much touted Foothills Trail begins here, marching 76 miles to Table Rock State Park or alternatively to Jones Gap State Park. Oconee State Park has two lakes for fishing and swimming. Nearby, the federally designated Wild and Scenic Chattooga River has outfitters ready to take you on guided whitewater trips.

The walk-in tent sites spur from the main campground near campsite 70. A pair of carts aids in toting gear back to the campsites from the parking area. Leave the walk-in parking area on a footpath. A scenic mountain forest of maple, hickory, oak, and white pine grows overhead. Smaller trees, mountain laurel, and cane grow as an understory. The trail splits and sites T-1 through T-10 are ahead. The hillside sites have been leveled, and all of the sites are well shaded and private, especially T-7. Campsite T-8 was my preference. Beyond campsite T-10, the walk-in access trail keeps forward to meet the Oconee Trail.

Campsites T-11 through T-15 are farther from the parking area. Follow a common path before reaching a level area, where spur trails lead downhill to each of the campsites, which are near the park's smaller lake. Campsite T-11 is in a mountain laurel thicket. Campsite T-12 is also in laurel but is closer to the lake. A small path leads to the water. T-13 has room to roam.

RATINGS

Beauty: ✿ ✿ ✿ ✿
Privacy: ✿ ✿ ✿
Spaciousness: ✿ ✿ ✿ ✿
Quiet: ✿ ✿ ✿ ✿
Security: ✿ ✿ ✿ ✿ ✿
Cleanliness: ✿ ✿ ✿ ✿

T-14 is very close to the water and is well shaded by white pines. T-15 is the most private of them all, and is also the farthest from the parking area.

The main campground may scare you. The sites are mostly small and crowded but they do have water and electricity. A hard look around may yield a few nice sites, but overall the sites don't begin to compare with the walk-in tent sites. I would rather not stay here if I couldn't get a walk-in tent site, which is most likely on a holiday weekend. The main campground does have a recreation building handy for rainy days. The Trading Post, a small camp store, is open during the warm season. Sites should be available most weekends other than holidays and all weekdays. The last two weekends in October see an upsurge in traffic from leaf watchers.

Oddly, a little putt-putt course abuts the campground and is the only artificial diversion around. The lakes are a nicer alternative than putt-putt, but the mountains and trails running over them are the real attraction. At the lakes, the park rents johnboats, canoes, kayaks, and paddleboats for tooling around or fishing for catfish, bream, and bass. No private boats are allowed. Trout are stocked here during winter, and a swim area is located on the larger lake.

It only seems fitting that this lake would have a trail around it—the Lake Trail—since this park is very trail oriented. The Old Waterwheel Trail leads to the site where the Civilian Conservation Corps, who originally developed this park in the 1930s, built a waterwheel to pump water. The Hidden Falls Trail leads to a 60-foot waterfall. Start your hike to Hidden Falls on the Foothills Trail, which leads down to the Chattooga River and beyond. The Tamassee Knob Trail also spurs from the Foothills Trail. Here, you reach a rock outcrop with far-reaching views to the west. You can actually connect to all these trails, except the Lake Trail, from the Oconee Trail, which runs directly by the walk-in camping area. A trail map is available at the park office, where you can see some neat relics from the CCC days.

If you haven't rafted the Chattooga here's your

KEY INFORMATION

ADDRESS: Oconee State Park
624 State Park Road
Mountain Rest, SC
29664

OPERATED BY: South Carolina State
Parks

INFORMATION: (864) 638-5353;
www.southcarolina
parks.com

OPEN: Year-round

SITES: 15 walk-in tent sites,
140 others

EACH SITE HAS: Walk-in sites have
picnic table, fire
grate, tent pad,
lantern post; others
also have water and
electricity

ASSIGNMENT: First come, first
served and by reservation; walk-in tent
sites are first come,
first served only

REGISTRATION: At campground
trading post if open,
otherwise ranger
will come by and
register you

FACILITIES: Hot showers, flush
toilets, water spigots,
camp store in season

PARKING: At walk-in camper
parking area and at
campsites

FEE: Walk-in sites $8 per
night, others $16 per
night

ELEVATION: 1,825 feet

RESTRICTIONS: Pets: On leash only
Fires: In fire rings
only
Alcohol: Prohibited
Vehicles: Two per
campsite
Other: 14-day stay
limit

MAP

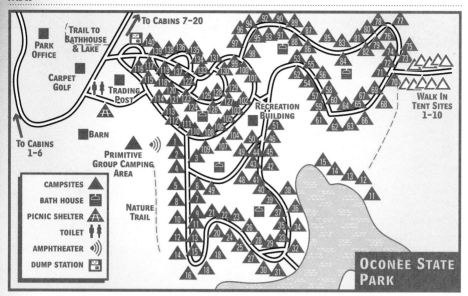

GETTING THERE

From Walhalla, drive north on South Carolina 28 north for 8.5 miles to SC 107. Turn right on SC 107 and follow it 2.5 miles to the state park, on your right.

chance. The river is less than 10 miles distant and several outfitters are located by the river. The park office has a list of outfitters and directions to the Chattooga. This has been one of my favorite rivers for a long time, whether it be for backpacking, fishing, tent camping, or rafting. You might say that the Chattooga River and Oconee State Park, among other places, put the "gold" in South Carolina's Golden Corner.

SADLERS CREEK STATE RECREATION AREA

THIS STATE RECREATION AREA is situated on a peninsula with five fingers of land extending into Lake Hartwell. This park seemingly has more "shoreland" than "inland." So, it comes as no surprise that much of the campground is along the shore as well. The park covers the entire peninsula, adding an "island effect" to this getaway on Lake Hartwell. Outdoor recreation is primarily centered on the lake, but the park does offer some activities for landlubbers.

The 37 campsites are spread over two loops. Most South Carolina state recreation area campgrounds have three or more times the number of campsites. The small number of sites at Sadlers Creek keeps the park quieter and improves the camping experience. However, Sadlers Creek once had more campsites, but they were removed, skewing the campsite numbering system.

Reach the first campground road, a gravel road dipping right toward the lake. There are 14 campsites along the road, although a sign indicates otherwise. The first few sites are somewhat small and strung out on either side of the road. Reach waterfront sites that have a good view but with gravel floors that could make staking a tent tough. Bring the mallet. Campsites 33 and 34 are the best waterfront sites in this area. A heated bath house on this loop makes those cold mornings tolerable.

The second camping area has 23 campsites. The sites are spread along a loop road descending toward Lake Hartwell. Ten sites in the inside of this loop are designated tent sites. They are a little small, but are well shaded by shagbark hickory, oaks, dogwood, and shortleaf pine. These first seven designated tent sites have been leveled. T-5 is larger than most other tent sites. The main loop curves around and comes to waterfront sites, which have water and electricity, and

> *Ten of the 47 sites in this campground on Hartwell Lake are designated tent sites.*

RATINGS

Beauty: ✿ ✿ ✿
Privacy: ✿ ✿ ✿
Spaciousness: ✿ ✿
Quiet: ✿ ✿ ✿
Security: ✿ ✿ ✿ ✿ ✿
Cleanliness: ✿ ✿ ✿ ✿

ADDRESS: Sadlers Creek State
Recreation Area
940 Sadlers Creek
Road
Anderson, SC 29626

OPERATED BY: South Carolina State
Parks

INFORMATION: (864) 226-8950;
www.southcarolina
parks.com

OPEN: Year-round

SITES: 10 tent sites, 37
others

EACH SITE HAS: Tent sites have picnic
table, upright grill,
rock fire ring, others
also have water and
electricity

ASSIGNMENT: First come, first
served; no reserva-
tions

REGISTRATION: Ranger will come by
and register you

FACILITIES: Hot showers, flush
toilets, water spigots,
pay phone

PARKING: At campsites only

FEE: Tent sites $7.50 per
night, others $15 per
night

ELEVATION: 690 feet

RESTRICTIONS: Pets: On leash only
Fires: In fire rings
only
Alcohol: Prohibited
Vehicles: Two per
site
Other: 14-day stay
limit

are thus more expensive. Campsites 54 through 59 are the best waterfront sites. The loop then curves away from the lake, passing three more designated tent sites. These are small and lack the plant growth privacy between sites that the first seven tent sites have. While other lakefront campgrounds are packed, Sadlers Creek fills only on summer holiday weekends and on an occasional ideal weather weekend. Sites are available anytime during the week.

Large Lake Hartwell is the big drawing card here. The name Hart and Hartwell are spread all over the place in these parts. Nancy Hart, a Revolutionary War patriot, who by dint of her service to a fledgling United States, earned the honor of having Hart County and Hartwell, Georgia, named for her. Later, Hartwell Dam and Lake were derived from her name as well.

The lake is a huge impoundment, covering 56,000 acres, enough to hold a fish or two, or allow a little room for a water-skier or swimmer. Lake Hartwell has 962 miles of shoreline, where prior to the dam, the Tugaloo and Seneca rivers once flowed together to form the Savannah River. Sadlers Creek State Recreation Area is not far from the point where these two rivers met to form the Savannah. Of course, this confluence is now underwater. This abundance of water can come in handy when summer hits this part of the South, when folks hit the water to cool off. There are no organized swimming areas at Sadlers Creek, but with nothing but water around you, finding a swimming locale is easy here, as is bank fishing. You can also drop your craft into the water from the park boat ramp.

The park prides itself on their entry-level mountain bike trail. It winds for 7.8 miles through the peninsula. This trail, which starts near the campground, is also open to hikers. Five miles of paved park roads attract other more casual bicyclers. The Pine Grove Nature Trail is a good, half-mile walk. And that's about all the trails you can put on this five-fingered peninsula jutting into Lake Hartwell.

MAP

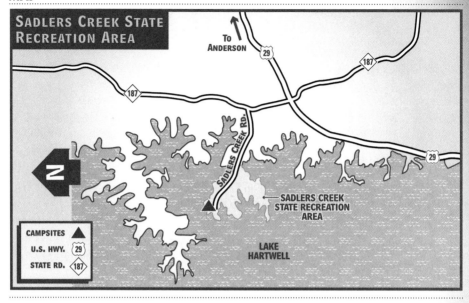

SADLERS CREEK STATE
RECREATION AREA

To
ANDERSON

187

SADLERS CREEK RD.

SADLERS CREEK
STATE RECREATION
AREA

LAKE
HARTWELL

CAMPSITES

U.S. HWY. 29

STATE RD. 187

GETTING THERE

From Anderson, take US 29
south for 15 miles to SC 187.
Turn right, and take SC 187
north for 0.8 miles to reach
Sadlers Creek Road. Turn left
on Sadlers Creek Road. Follow Sadlers Creek Road for
1.2 miles to enter the park.

TABLE ROCK STATE PARK

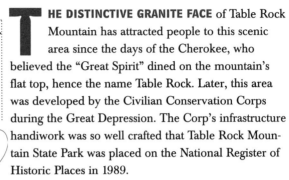

The wide variety of attractions at this state park will make your stay worthwhile.

THE DISTINCTIVE GRANITE FACE of Table Rock Mountain has attracted people to this scenic area since the days of the Cherokee, who believed the "Great Spirit" dined on the mountain's flat top, hence the name Table Rock. Later, this area was developed by the Civilian Conservation Corps during the Great Depression. The Corp's infrastructure handiwork was so well crafted that Table Rock Mountain State Park was placed on the National Register of Historic Places in 1989.

Not that this park needed humankind's imprint to be special. Waterfalls, deep forests, and rock outcrops adorned the mountains long before the 3,083 acres became a state park in 1935. The facilities just make it user-friendly for tent campers.

The campground suffices for a two- or three-day stay, but is not a destination unto itself. The main camping area has 75 sites spread on two loops in open rolling woods that have suffered the ravages of many storms. These storms made pulp of the pine trees that once dotted the campground. In addition, little is left of the understory, minimizing privacy. It's strange to see a campground with electric and water hookups at each campsite but no elaborate site shaping or defined tent pads. But don't let that scare you away—only 20 of the sites are designated pull-through, which translates to RV.

The first eight sites lie along the approach road and are very open. They are among the 25 sites that can be reserved. Once inside the loop, campsites are placed fairly close together. Three bath houses with flush toilets and hot showers are evenly dispersed among the campsites, except for sites on the approach road. Degrees of sun, shade, and slope vary from campsite to campsite. Plenty of level, shaded sites are available. Expect the best ones to be taken during the weekends.

RATINGS

Beauty: ☆ ☆ ☆
Privacy: ☆ ☆ ☆
Spaciousness: ☆ ☆
Quiet: ☆ ☆ ☆
Security: ☆ ☆ ☆ ☆ ☆
Cleanliness: ☆ ☆ ☆ ☆ ☆

Located in thicker woods on a dead-end road, the overflow area may actually be preferable to the main camping area if you like less hustle and bustle. The 25 sites are spread along a loop and share a single bath house in the loop's center with flush toilets.

At Table Rock, the campground is just a place to rest and eat between activities. Miniature golf, a gift shop, and concessions open on Memorial Day weekend.

Two lakes lie within the park's confines. Pinnacle Lake finds summertime campers relaxing on its beach or jumping off the high and low diving boards into the clear, cool waters; canoers fishing for bass, bream, or catfish; and pedal boaters taking scenic rides atop the lake's 36 acres.

If water is not your thing, get together with the full-time park naturalist. Daily programs are offered during summer. The Table Rock Nature Center has displays that detail the natural history of the region. Children can have fun playing putt-putt.

None of the above would be there if it weren't for the natural beauty of Table Rock. And the best way to enjoy these South Carolina mountain lands is on foot. A 10-mile trail network emanates from the Nature Center. The 3.4-mile Table Rock Trail lives up to its National Recreation Trail status. It leads upward among giant boulders to Pinnacle Ridge at Panther Gap. From Panther Gap, the trail climbs the steps of the Governor's Rock to reach the top of Table Rock at 3 miles. Hike another half mile to a wide view of the South Carolina countryside.

The Pinnacle Mountain Trail is very challenging. It passes Mill Creek Falls and Bald Rock on the way to the 3,425-foot peak, the park's highest point. A 2-mile connector trail links Pinnacle Mountain and Table Rock trails. The Carrick Creek Nature Trail offers a shorter 1.8-mile loop through forest characteristic of this worthwhile park.

KEY INFORMATION

ADDRESS:	Table Rock State Park 158 East Ellison Lane Pickens, SC 29671
OPERATED BY:	South Carolina State Parks
INFORMATION:	(864) 878-9813; www.southcarolina parks.com
OPEN:	Year-round
SITES:	100
EACH SITE HAS:	Water, electricity, picnic table, fire ring
ASSIGNMENT:	25 sites by reservation; 75 sites first come, first served
REGISTRATION:	At camp store, April to October; register with ranger during the rest of year; reserve by phone, (864) 878-9818
FACILITIES:	Water, hot showers, camp store, laundry
PARKING:	At campsites only
FEE:	$17.69 per night after tax; $1.50 parking fee in summer
ELEVATION:	1,160 feet
RESTRICTIONS:	**Pets:** On leash only **Fires:** In fire rings only **Alcohol:** Not allowed **Vehicles:** None **Other:** 14-day stay limit

MAP

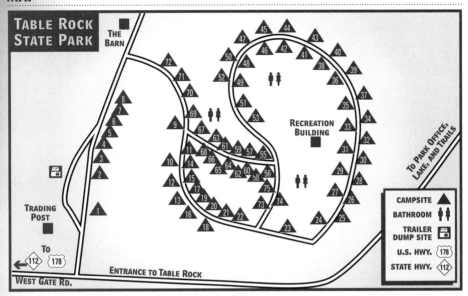

TABLE ROCK STATE PARK

THE BARN

72 71 70 69 67 63 68 61 59 57 55 66 64 65 62 60 58 56

8 7 6 5 4 3 2 1

TRADING POST

To
112 178

WEST GATE RD.

ENTRANCE TO TABLE ROCK

47 45 44 50 46 42 43 48 41 40 52 49 38 39 51 35 36 37 53 34 33 32 31 30 29 28 27 26 25 24

RECREATION BUILDING

10 14 12 15 11 17 13 19 16 20 21 22 18 75 73 74 23

TO PARK OFFICE, LAKE, AND TRAILS

CAMPSITE	▲
BATHROOM	♀♂
TRAILER DUMP SITE	🚽
U.S. HWY.	178
STATE HWY.	112

GETTING THERE

From Pickens drive north on US 178 for 9 miles. Turn right on SC 11 and follow it for 4.4 miles to West Gate Road. The park is a half mile up West Gate Road.

SOUTH CAROLINA **MIDLANDS**

BRICK HOUSE CAMPGROUND

TALK ABOUT TRANSITION—one minute I was zipping along I-26 and the next minute I was at Brick House campground. The place was so quiet I could hear myself breathe. The rushing down the interstate was exactly what I was trying to get away from. The serene atmosphere and quaint natural setting of Brick House was exactly the setting tent campers look for. Brick House delivered, so much so I just hung around the campsite all day reveling in the crisp and clear fall air that had swept over the South Carolina Midlands. The next day I hiked the nearby Buncombe Trail, but a mountain bike would've been an even better venue for traveling this trail. I was regrettably bikeless. However, mountain bikers are discovering and enjoying this path in ever increasing numbers.

The Enoree District of the Sumter National Forest is just a short drive up I-26 from Columbia. So it makes sense that the Buncombe Trail is catching on. But the lack of use at Brick House Campground is surprising. Sure, a few equestrians, hunters, and family campers find their way here, but this place can be a nice base camp for trail enthusiasts, too. Despite being only 4 miles from the interstate, Brick House seems a world away.

After passing the Buncombe Trailhead, enter the campground loop, where tall pines form the forest superstory. Elms, dogwoods, sweetgums, and other hardwoods grow beneath the taller evergreens. The forest floor is littered with pine needles and pointy sweetgum balls.

There is little brush between campsites, but campsite privacy isn't as much of an issue as you would think. Since this campground rarely if ever fills, you likely won't have a neighbor next to you. Campsites 1 and 2 are situated together, and act as a double site.

> *This quiet campground is base camp for those traveling the Buncombe Trail.*

RATINGS

Beauty: ✰ ✰ ✰
Privacy: ✰ ✰
Spaciousness: ✰ ✰ ✰ ✰
Quiet: ✰ ✰ ✰ ✰
Security: ✰ ✰ ✰
Cleanliness: ✰ ✰ ✰

KEY INFORMATION

ADDRESS: Brick House Campground
20 Work Center Road
Whitmire, SC 29178

OPERATED BY: U.S. Forest Service

INFORMATION: (864) 427-9858;
www.fs.fed.us/r8/fms

OPEN: Year-round

SITES: 23

EACH SITE HAS: Picnic table, fire ring, most also have lantern post

ASSIGNMENT: First come, first served; no reservations

REGISTRATION: Self-registration on-site

FACILITIES: Water spigots, vault toilets

PARKING: At campsites only

FEE: $5 per night

ELEVATION: 450 feet

RESTRICTIONS: Pets: On leash only
Fires: In fire rings only
Alcohol: At campsites only
Vehicles: Two per site
Other: 14-day stay limit

The woods are sparse behind these camps due to cutting from a pine beetle infestation, but most pines in the campground loop have been spared. Pass a water spigot and come to large open sites on the outside the loop. A stone marker for the Youth Conservation Corps, who rehabilitated this campground and the Buncombe Trail, is next to the road. Campsite 12 is purely in pines. Curve around to reach the shady campsites.

Notice the white-banded trees near some campsites. These are where occasional horse campers can tie their animals. The terrain slopes away from the campground as the loop turns back toward Brick House Road. Some open sites lie on the inside of the loop. Come to a group of three shady sites at the campground's end. This is where I stayed, in 23. Two new "sweet-smelling technology" vault toilets serve the campground.

You may notice blue blazes on trees running behind campsite 13. This is the Buncombe Trail. You can pick it up there, or start at the trailhead, located just a short piece down Brick House Road that you passed on the way in. The Buncombe Trail, open to hikers, bikers, and equestrians, is broken into colored segments of different lengths. It circles the Headley Creek watershed through environments typical of the Piedmont. The Red Trail cuts across the main loop, allowing two loop trips of 9 and 12 miles respectively. Hikers, mountain bikers, and equestrians are welcome to enjoy this trail. Trail maps are posted at signboards in the campground and the trailhead. South Carolina's master path, the Palmetto Trail, runs in conjunction with part of the Buncombe Trail. My recommendation is to bike the path. I wish I'd had my two-wheeler, though the camping trip was very rewarding, and that is what tent camping is all about.

MAP

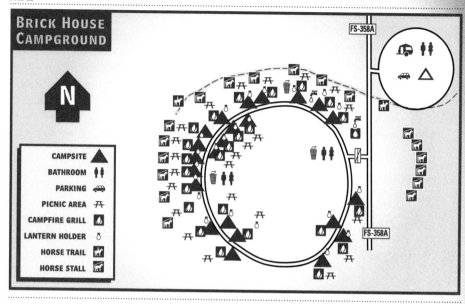

BRICK HOUSE CAMPGROUND

CAMPSITE	▲
BATHROOM	♀♂
PARKING	🚗
PICNIC AREA	⛾
CAMPFIRE GRILL	🔥
LANTERN HOLDER	🔦
HORSE TRAIL	🐎
HORSE STALL	🐎

FS-358A

FS-358A

GETTING THERE

From Exit 60 on I-26 near Clinton, take SC 66 east for 3.6 miles to Brick House Road. Turn right on Brick House Road, Forest Road 358, and follow it for 0.5 miles to reach the campground, on your right.

CALHOUN FALLS
STATE RECREATION
AREA

The awesome walk-in tent sites here are so good they should serve as models for other parks to follow!

DON'T LOOK FOR SOME BIG WATERFALL when you come to this lakeside recreation area. Before the damming of Richard B. Russell Lake, the Savannah River once flowed free. At high water, a river rapid on the Savannah River, near where the Calhoun family resided, resembled a waterfall. Now, Calhoun Falls is just the name of a town and nearby state recreation area, centered on large Lake Russell. The Army Corps of Engineers developed this impoundment, the middle of three consecutive large reservoirs damming the Savannah River. Part of their work was on Calhoun Falls State Recreation Area, which they turned over to the South Carolina state park system to manage. The walk-in tent sites here are so good they should serve as models for other parks to follow.

Quality campsites are expensive to build, and the Army Corps of Engineers spared no expense here. It is evident in the fixtures of every campsite you see, with first-rate fire grates, picnic tables, lantern posts, and more. The walk-in tent sites are near Campground 2. The first set of walk-in tent sites is T-5 through T-0. Dip into thick woods and a streamside hollow. T-5 is in a flat beside the hollow. Landscaping timbers have been laid into the hillside to level the campsites, which have a sand floor. Cross two footbridges and reach T-4. The site is very shady and has a walkway to the lake. The path leaves the hollow and reaches campsites overlooking an arm of the lake. T-3 is more open but is shaded by water oak, cedar, and a few other trees. Bring a canopy during mid-summer for sun protection. T-2 directly overlooks the water. Campsite T-1 is set on a point. Shade is limited but the water panorama is appealing. Campsite T-0 is over a hill and has the maximum solitude. The walk from the parking area to T-0 is about 140 yards.

RATINGS

Beauty: ✩ ✩ ✩ ✩
Privacy: ✩ ✩ ✩ ✩
Spaciousness: ✩ ✩ ✩ ✩
Quiet: ✩ ✩ ✩ ✩
Security: ✩ ✩ ✩ ✩ ✩
Cleanliness: ✩ ✩ ✩

The second walk-in area is home to campsites T-6 through T-13, located on the upper end of a cove. Campsites T-6 and T-7 are so close to the parking area as to almost lose their walk-in status. That is not to say they are bad—they aren't—the camps are directly on the water. Campsites T-8 and T-9 are on the water but are more shaded. T-10 has easy access to the parking area but not to the lake. T-11 is thickly shaded but is off the lake. Cross footbridges to reach T-12. It is on the water, shaded, and highly recommended. T-13, a shady site, is the farthest from the parking area. A path from T-13 leads to the water. All campsites here, including the walk-in tent sites, are reservable. Oddly, the walk-in tent sites generally fill only on holiday weekends. An outdoor shower, water spigots, and vault toilets are located in the immediate campground vicinity. Tent campers can use the showers at the other campgrounds.

Two other large campgrounds serve the park, Campground 1 and Campground 2. They are leveled, landscaped, and well thought out, mixing pull-through sites with pull-up sites for RVs and tent campers who wish to have on-site water and electricity. A look at these two lakeside camping areas shows that no expense was spared here either. Campground 1 is closed during the off-season.

The developed recreation areas are nice too. The beach house for the lake's swim area is beyond elaborate for a park structure. Tennis courts and a basketball court are located near the beach house. The Cedar Bluff Nature Trail leaves from near the beach house and makes a 1.75-mile loop.

Most of the other recreation opportunities center on Richard B. Russell Lake. The recreation area has its own marina, boat ramp, dock, and tackle shop. The lake was named after a Georgia politician, to offset the naming of another lake located downstream for the venerable South Carolina politician Strom Thurmond. The Savannah River forms much of the border between South Carolina and Georgia. Russell Lake covers 26,000 acres, plenty of room to endeavor in the water sport of your choice. If you don't have a boat, you can cast your line from one of the two park fishing

ADDRESS: Calhoun Falls State Recreation Area 46 Maintenance Park Road Calhoun Falls, SC 29628

OPERATED BY: South Carolina State Parks

INFORMATION: (864) 447-8267; www.southcarolina parks.com

OPEN: Year-round

SITES: 14 walk-in tent sites, 86 others

EACH SITE HAS: Walk-in sites have picnic tables, fire ring, lantern post, cooking table; others also have water and electricity

ASSIGNMENT: First come, first served and by reservation

REGISTRATION: At tackle shop

FACILITIES: Hot showers, flush toilets, vault toilets, water spigots

PARKING: At walk-in camper parking area and at campsites

FEE: Walk-in tent sites $9 per night, others $18 per night

ELEVATION: 500 feet

RESTRICTIONS: Pets: On leash only Fires: In fire rings only Alcohol: Prohibited Vehicles: Two per campsite Other: 14-day stay limit

MAP

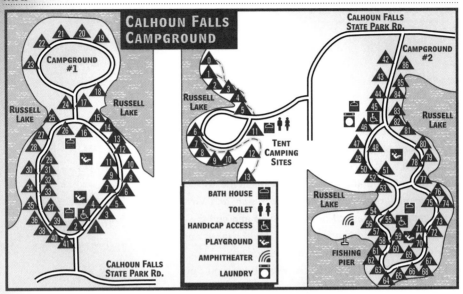

GETTING THERE

From Abbeville, take SC 72 west for 15 miles to the town of Calhoun Falls and SC 81. Turn right on SC 81 and follow it 1.1 miles to the state recreation area, on your left.

piers. One is located near the walk-in area by campsite 56 of Campground 2. The other pier is by the boat ramp. Just remember, one water feature you won't see at this quality destination is a waterfall.

KINGS MOUNTAIN
STATE PARK

Blacksburg

DID YOU KNOW that more Revolutionary War battles took place in South Carolina than in any other state? The Battle of Kings Mountain, which took place on October 7, 1780, is considered the turning point for the Americans in the South. Frontiersmen from the Carolinas, Tennessee, and Virginia gathered to defeat Lord Cornwallis and end the British advance into North Carolina. The Loyalists and English Army were forced to retreat back to Charleston, ultimately to lose the war. Today, you can visit this battlefield, known as Kings Mountain National Military Park, and pitch your tent at the adjacent Kings Mountain State Park, which functions as the recreational counterpart to the battlefield. Here, you can hike, swim, fish, and enjoy yet more American history beyond the battlefield.

Campsites at the state park campground are widespread among pines and oaks. Passing the Trading Post, a small campground store, the ridge top camping area slopes away from the campsites. The first large loop has 75 sites, which are shared by tent campers, pop ups and RVs. The second major loop has the balance of the campsites, including walk-in tent sites. The tent camper parking area is near site 82. Beyond the parking area and along the loop, sites are far enough in the woods to lend a rustic atmosphere, but not so far back that you'll feel like a mine mule after setting up camp. The understory is much thicker among the tent sites, with brush and smaller trees complementing the shady forest. Descend along a ridge line between two narrow hollows to find site T-1, which is closest to the parking area. T-2 and T-3 are next to a dry streambed. A trail leads past campsite T-4. As the loop begins to curve back uphill. reach campsite T-5, which is a bit sloped. Campsite T-6 has many pines, and has a water spigot near it. I would be proud to pitch my tent at T-7

> *This large state park complements the adjacent Revolutionary War battlefield.*

RATINGS

Beauty: ✪ ✪ ✪
Privacy: ✪ ✪ ✪
Spaciousness: ✪ ✪ ✪ ✪
Quiet: ✪ ✪ ✪
Security: ✪ ✪ ✪ ✪ ✪
Cleanliness: ✪ ✪ ✪ ✪

ADDRESS: Kings Mountain State Park
1277 Park Road
Blacksburg, SC
29702

OPERATED BY: South Carolina State Parks

INFORMATION: (803) 222-3209; www.southcarolinaparks.com

OPEN: Year-round

SITES: 10 walk-in tent sites, 116 other sites

EACH SITE HAS: Walk-in sites have picnic table, tent pad, fire ring; others also have water and electricity but no tent pad

ASSIGNMENT: First come, first served; no reservations

REGISTRATION: At campground Trading Post April to October; ranger will come by and register rest of year

FACILITIES: Hot showers, flush toilets, laundry

PARKING: At walk-in tent parking and at campsites

FEE: $8 per night walk-in tent sites, $16 per night other sites

ELEVATION: 750 feet

RESTRICTIONS: Pets: On leash only
Fires: In fire rings only
Alcohol: Prohibited
Vehicles: Two per site
Other: 14-day stay limit

or T-8. The loop curves back toward the parking area, making campsites T-9 and T-10 easily accessible.

A campground host assists campers during the warmer months. Numerous bath houses are evenly spread among the loops, including one near the tent camper's parking area. A recreation building at the campground makes rainy days more livable. The campground sees its most traffic during spring and fall, but only fills on major summer holidays and Pioneer Days in September. Pioneer Days is centered around a historic homestead at the state park that replicates an 1840s farm. The festival features crafts, music, and a muzzle loaders competition. A trail connects the campground to the living history farm. The campground also sees some traffic from I-85 travelers, but walk-in tent campers can nearly always get a campsite.

The state park offers 7,000 acres, and combined with the 3,000 acres of the military park, makes for a lot of roaming space in the shadow of Charlotte. Two lakes add to the attractive park terrain. Lake Crawford covers 15-acres and has a swimming area for hot days. Lake York is larger at 65 acres and offers johnboats for rent, so anglers can vie for bass and bream. Basketball and volleyball courts, and a carpet golf course are near the campground.

I really enjoyed the hiking trail that connects the state park to the military park. The path makes a 16-mile loop, and has backcountry campsites amid its ridges and bottomlands, where clear streams flow. I wasn't able to make the whole loop, but the fall colors were phenomenal during my early November stay. If you don't feel like walking to the nearby Kings Mountain battlefield, just make the short drive, where you can stop at the visitor center and check out the museum and a film explaining the battle. Then, take the 1.5-mile self-guiding loop trail around the battlefield, and appreciate one of South Carolina's many Revolutionary War sites.

MAP

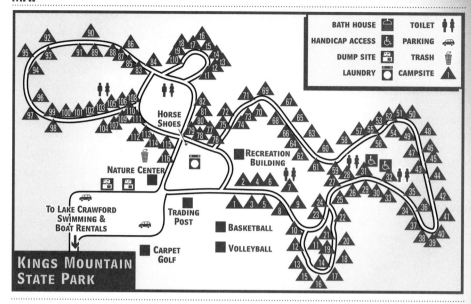

KINGS MOUNTAIN STATE PARK

To Lake Crawford
Swimming &
Boat Rentals

NATURE CENTER

HORSE SHOES

TRADING POST

CARPET GOLF

BASKETBALL

VOLLEYBALL

RECREATION BUILDING

GETTING THERE

From Exit 8, Kings Mountain, on I-85 just north of the North Carolina/South Carolina border, take NC 161 south for 5 miles, leaving North Carolina en route. Turn right on Park Road and follow it into the state park.

LEROY'S FERRY
CAMPGROUND

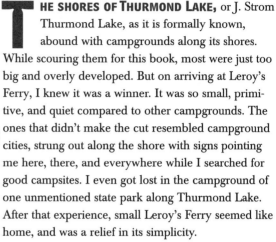

> *This is the most primitive campground on the shores of Thurmond Lake.*

THE SHORES OF THURMOND LAKE, or J. Strom Thurmond Lake, as it is formally known, abound with campgrounds along its shores. While scouring them for this book, most were just too big and overly developed. But on arriving at Leroy's Ferry, I knew it was a winner. It was so small, primitive, and quiet compared to other campgrounds. The ones that didn't make the cut resembled campground cities, strung out along the shore with signs pointing me here, there, and everywhere while I searched for good campsites. I even got lost in the campground of one unmentioned state park along Thurmond Lake. After that experience, small Leroy's Ferry seemed like home, and was a relief in its simplicity.

And Leroy's Ferry is simple. This Army Corps of Engineers campground is more about what it doesn't have than what it does have. It doesn't have a ranger station, confusing signs, hordes of bustling campers, or cars and trailers constantly coming and going. Furthermore, it doesn't have much to do in the way of organized recreation. There are no trails to hike or bike, no nature interpretive centers, no boats to rent, no piers from which to fish. The only amenity, in addition to the campground, is a boat launch. You have two choices here, make your own fun on Lake Thurmond, or just relax at the campground, which is a fine thing in itself. And for five bucks a day, the price is right. Making your own fun could also include bank fishing or swimming on the shoreline.

Just because this campground is primitive doesn't mean it's not well taken care of. The Army Corps of Engineers generally takes good care of its property, which ultimately belongs to us. Reach the end of the dead-end road and pass the fee station that is near the pump well. A gravel road leads right a quarter mile to campsites 4 through 1. Reach the campsites in reverse

RATINGS

Beauty: ☆ ☆ ☆
Privacy: ☆ ☆ ☆ ☆ ☆
Spaciousness: ☆ ☆ ☆ ☆
Quiet: ☆ ☆ ☆
Security: ☆ ☆ ☆
Cleanliness: ☆ ☆ ☆

order. The hillside slopes toward the lake but the campsites are mostly level. Campsite 4 is large and overlooks the lake. Campsite 3 is a good distance away in thick woods. Pine grows highest above these sites, followed by a thick bank of winged elm, sweetgum, and oak. Smaller trees and brush create more than ample campsite privacy. Campsite 2 is less shady. Campsite 1 is close to the lake.

Return to the main road that shortly splits. The paved road leading left dead ends at the boat ramp. A second gravel road splits right. It has campsites 10 through 5. Campsite 10 is large and is closest to the boat ramp. Campsite 9 is well above the lake while sites 8 and 7 are separated by thick woods, but open toward Lake Thurmond. I stayed in campsite 6 because it provided good afternoon shade on a hot summer day. Campsite 5 is at the road's end. Informal trails lead a short distance from these campsites to the lake. Although the campground has 10 sites, it fills only on holiday weekends. Other than then, you should get a site.

People come here for water recreation, whether it be fishing, boating, skiing, or swimming. And Lake Thurmond is a huge recreation destination. Completed in 1954, the lake now hosts 7 million visitors annually. But it doesn't seem that way at Leroy's Ferry. After all, a tent camper can still find a little solitude along the 1,200 miles of shoreline here. The lake also has over 100 islands that add a scenic touch to the impoundment. It seems the lake also has 100 campgrounds, but you will likely find that the few sites at Leroy's Ferry offer the best in tent camping.

KEY INFORMATION

ADDRESS: Leroy's Ferry Campground Route 1, Box 6 Clarks Hill, SC 29821

OPERATED BY: Army Corps of Engineers

INFORMATION: (800) 533-3478; www.sas.usace.army.mil/lakes/thurmond

OPEN: Year-round

SITES: 10

EACH SITE HAS: Picnic table, fire grate, lantern post, most have upright grill

ASSIGNMENT: First come, first served; no reservations

REGISTRATION: Self-registration on site

FACILITIES: Pump well, vault toilets

PARKING: At campsites only

FEE: $5 per night

ELEVATION: 340 feet

RESTRICTIONS: **Pets:** On leash only
Fires: In fire rings only
Alcohol: At campsites only
Vehicles: None
Other: 14-day stay limit

MAP

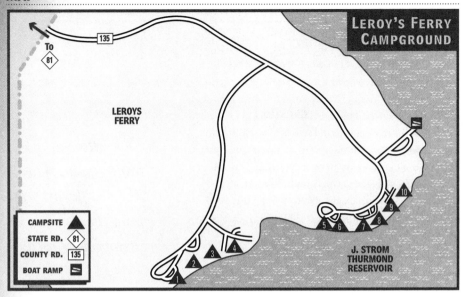

LEROY'S FERRY CAMPGROUND

135

To 81

LEROYS FERRY

J. STROM THURMOND RESERVOIR

CAMPSITE
STATE RD. 81
COUNTY RD. 135
BOAT RAMP

GETTING THERE

From McCormick, take SC
28 north for 7 miles to SC 81,
veer left, staying with SC 81
north for 5.5 miles to the
hamlet of Willington. Turn
left at the signed turn for
Leroy's Ferry Campground,
going just a few feet over
defunct railroad track, then
immediately turn right on SC
196. Follow 196 for 0.5 miles,
then turn left on SC 135 and
follow it 4 miles to dead end
at the campground.

LICK FORK LAKE CAMPGROUND

CAMPGROUNDS AND RECREATION areas come in all sizes. Lick Fork Lake is a mere 12 acres, small in size compared to most impoundments, especially in comparison to nearby Strom Thurmond Lake. Lick Fork Lake campground only has ten sites, which is just about the right size to handle this lake. Located in the surprisingly deep valley of Lick Fork (but only 10 miles from a town), the area exudes a close, intimate feel as if you are in the middle of nowhere, a good thing. The "no-gas-motors" rule on Lick Fork Lake and the widespread campsites means chirping birds and maybe some kids swimming in the clear water will be your only background noise.

I really like this campground. The campsites are spacious and spread out far from one another. They are incorporated into a hilly setting with some leveling and stonework that makes the sites both attractive and "campable." Oaks and pines shade the campsites. A gravel road dips toward Lick Fork Lake, passing a water spigot to reach campsites 1 and 2. These are on mostly level terrain. Sand has been spread in individual camping areas, which have a separate tent pad. Campsites 3 through 5 are built into a slope. Landscaping stones held together with concrete form leveling walls resulting in two-tiered sites. As the gravel road curves toward the lake, reach campsite 6 that overlooks the lake from across the road. Then come to the most favored campsites, 7 through 9. These sites directly overlook Lick Fork Lake, which is just a short down-slope walk away. Campsite 9 is on a point just above the lake's fishing pier. The road then curves away from the lake into a hollow. The final campsite here, 10, is usually occupied by the campground host.

The campground, with so much area for so few sites, has four vault toilets. The small number of campsites does make it fill quickly at times, especially on

> *This little valley campground seems like a different world from the surrounding area.*

RATINGS

Beauty: ✿ ✿ ✿ ✿
Privacy: ✿ ✿ ✿
Spaciousness: ✿ ✿ ✿
Quiet: ✿ ✿ ✿ ✿
Security: ✿ ✿ ✿ ✿
Cleanliness: ✿ ✿ ✿

ADDRESS: Lick Fork Lake
Campground
810 Buncombe Street
Edgefield, SC 29824

OPERATED BY: South Carolina State
Parks

INFORMATION: (803) 637-5396;
www.fs.fed.us/r8/fms

OPEN: Year-round

SITES: 10

EACH SITE HAS: Picnic table, fire
ring, tent pad

ASSIGNMENT: First come, first
served; no reserva-
tions

REGISTRATION: Self-registration
on-site

FACILITIES: Cold showers, flush
toilets, vault toilets,
water spigots

PARKING: At campsites only

FEE: $7 per night

ELEVATION: 350 feet

RESTRICTIONS: Pets: On leash only
Fires: In fire rings
only
Alcohol: At camp-
sites only
Vehicles: None
Other: 14-day stay
limit

weekends during late spring and early summer. Then the heat kicks in and business dies down. Sites are available during the week any time of year. A camp-ground host is on duty most of the warm season and locks the campground gate at 10 p.m., which is a plus for camper security.

A newer rest room with cold showers overlooks the swim and picnic area. A picnic shelter here is a nice place to hang out during a summertime thunder-storm. Elaborate stonework has leveled parts of the picnic area, which overlooks a grassy lawn adjacent to the roped off swimming area. The swim area has a sandy bottom for clean-footed entry and exit of the pretty lake. A paved walkway with a quaint bridge connects the picnic area to a small fishing pier and the boat launch. As previously mentioned, no gas motors are allowed here where anglers vie primarily for cat-fish, but also largemouth bass and bream. The clear water and deep valley remind me of a small mountain lake, rather than a lake in the Midlands.

Two quality trails emanate from the boat launch area. The Lick Fork Trail circles around Lick Fork Lake, making a 2-mile circuit that emerges from the woods near the swim area. The Horn Creek Trail is longer at 5.7 miles. Mountain bikers really enjoy this route, though it does see its share of hikers. The path leaves the Lick Fork drainage then climbs over a ridge to dip into the Horn Creek drainage. From here, the path winds along Horn Creek before returning. It crosses forest roads three times, helping you track your progress. And Horn Creek may be about as far away as you want to get from this hideaway, tucked in the little valley of Lick Fork.

MAP

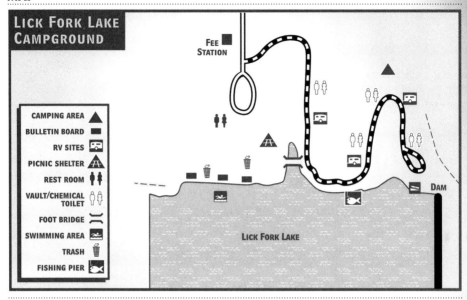

LICK FORK LAKE CAMPGROUND

FEE STATION

Legend:
- CAMPING AREA
- BULLETIN BOARD
- RV SITES
- PICNIC SHELTER
- REST ROOM
- VAULT/CHEMICAL TOILET
- FOOT BRIDGE
- SWIMMING AREA
- TRASH
- FISHING PIER

LICK FORK LAKE

DAM

GETTING THERE

From the Edgefield town square, head west on SC 23 for 8.3 miles to SC 230, Martintown Road. Veer left on SC 230 and follow it for 0.4 miles to Lick Fork Road. Turn left on Lick Fork Road and follow it for 2 miles to the campground, on your right.

PARSON'S MOUNTAIN

> *Tent campers will love this excellent national forest recreation area.*

PARSON'S **M**OUNTAIN **R**ECREATION **A**REA offers boating, swimming, fishing, and hiking along with an excellent campground in a rustic and well-kept setting. One goal of the U.S. Forest Service is to manage our national forests for public recreation. It is for this reason that areas like Parson's Mountain are developed. Under the multiple-use concept, the forest service also manages lands for watershed protection, timber harvesting, and wildlife enhancement among other things. Tent camper's benefit greatly from the recreation component of the multiple-use concept.

The roots of the recreation area were planted decades ago, when the Civilian Conservation Corps dammed Mountain Creek and developed the resulting shoreline, including the campground. The historic part of the recreation area, stonework and such, was left intact even after the area was modernized during recent years, including a bathhouse in the day-use area that complements the traditional campground. You will pass the day-use area before entering the campground. Campsites 1 and 3 are located on an arm of Parson's Mountain Lake and are the only lakeside campsites here. Oddly, the lakeside sites are lesser used than the main campground. Sweetgum, dogwood, pine, cedar, and elm comprise the forest overhead. Continue beyond a picnic area and enter the main part of the campground, on a hillside loop.

Starting with campsite 4, the sites are large. They are well separated from one another and have ample young trees between them for campsite privacy. Overhead shade from taller trees varies with the sites but is adequate at each camping area. Campsite 10 is of special note, as it is the most isolated site. Most sites on the loop's outside are set back in the woods, and a bathhouse centers the loop. Campsite 17 is closest to

RATINGS

Beauty: ✿ ✿ ✿ ✿
Privacy: ✿ ✿ ✿ ✿
Spaciousness: ✿ ✿ ✿ ✿
Quiet: ✿ ✿ ✿ ✿
Security: ✿ ✿ ✿ ✿
Cleanliness: ✿ ✿ ✿

the bathhouse. A short trail connects the main loop to the day-use area near campsite 20. A campground host is on duty during the warm season.

Twenty-three sites is a desirable number for a campground. The size keeps the campground generally quiet, but not so small that it fills too quickly. However, Parson's Mountain does fill on ideal spring and early summer weekends.

Just the right size, Parson's Mountain Lake covers 28 acres. The shoreline is pretty everywhere you look, whether it is the grassy picnic areas shaded by tall pines, or trees growing along the shoreline. No gas motors are allowed, and boaters will be pleased to know that the lake has a boat ramp. This makes boating or fishing for largemouth bass, bream, and catfish easy. An earthen pier on one side of the lake is where bank fishermen will be found. The primary day-use area has a designated swim beach, downhill from the modern bathhouse. It also has a large picnic shelter, which is good for seeking cover during summer thunderstorms.

Parson's Mountain Lake is not the only draw here. A hiking trail leads from near the lake spillway for 1.2 miles to the top of Parson's Mountain, where a fire tower stands. This out-and-back hike has a 400-foot elevation change, a big change in these parts, and offers a changing forestscape along the way. Unfortunately, the fire tower is closed. You can also see evidence of Civil-War era gold-mining along the trail. The Parson's Mountain OHV Trail is open to hikers, bikers, and motorized vehicles. The path makes a 12-mile loop south of the recreation area. It can be accessed by keeping east on Parson's Mountain Road, beyond the turn into the campground to Forest Road 515. Turn right on FR 515 to reach the trailhead past the road to the fire tower.

After a visit to Parson's Mountain, you will see that the forest service has had great success managing this part of the Sumter National Forest.

KEY INFORMATION

ADDRESS: Parson's Mountain 810 Buncombe Street Edgefield, SC 29824

OPERATED BY: U.S. Forest Service

INFORMATION: (803) 637-5396; www.fs.fed.us/r8/fms

OPEN: April through mid-December

SITES: 23

EACH SITE HAS: Picnic table, fire grate, tent pad, lantern post

ASSIGNMENT: First come, first served; no reservations

REGISTRATION: Self-registration on-site

FACILITIES: Hot showers, flush toilets, vault toilets, water spigots

PARKING: At campsites only

FEE: $7 per night

ELEVATION: 475 feet

RESTRICTIONS: Pets: On leash only
Fires: In fire rings only
Alcohol: Prohibited
Vehicles: Two per site
Other: 14-day stay limit

MAP

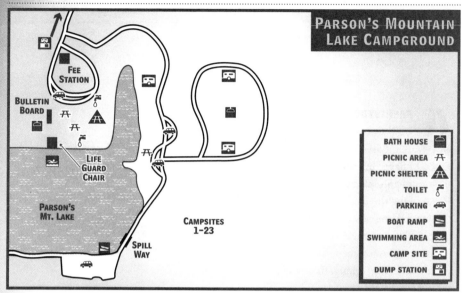

PARSON'S MOUNTAIN LAKE CAMPGROUND

FEE STATION

BULLETIN BOARD

LIFE GUARD CHAIR

PARSON'S MT. LAKE

SPILL WAY

CAMPSITES 1-23

BATH HOUSE	
PICNIC AREA	
PICNIC SHELTER	
TOILET	
PARKING	
BOAT RAMP	
SWIMMING AREA	
CAMP SITE	
DUMP STATION	

GETTING THERE

From Abbeville, take SC 72 west for 2 miles to SC 28. Turn left on SC 28 east and follow it for 2.3 miles to Parson's Mountain Road. Turn left on Parson's Mountain Road and follow it for 1.4 miles to Forest Road 514. Turn right on FR 514 and follow it 0.8 miles to reach the campground.

SAND HILLS
STATE FOREST

A PREHISTORIC SEA once covered what is now South Carolina, depositing sand over a wide area. Later, these seas retreated, leaving a region of deep, infertile hills of sand. Over time many plants and animals adapted to the Sand Hills, but settlers farming the land couldn't thrive as nature could. The state eventually acquired the land and now manages 46,000-acre Sand Hills State Forest. Here, tent campers can enjoy the activities of the forest, such as mountain biking, hiking, fishing and exploring the unique ecosystem.

By the way, the camping is free here, but you do need a permit from the forest office. And you get to camp on a hill so big it's called a mountain, Sugarloaf Mountain. Height is relative here on the edge of the Midlands, but views can be had when looking toward the coastal plain in parts of the forest.

Enter the campground via Mountain Road, dipping to Mountain Pond, a small but pretty impoundment of 10 acres. To your right are two large picnic shelters, made of wood and stone, flanked by campsites 1-A and 1-B. Campers can use these rustic shelters, which overlook Mountain Pond. Oaks, dogwoods, and pines shade the campsites, though the trees are widely separated in the area. Cross over the pond dam. Campsite 2 has a shelter and also overlooks the lake. Begin to climb Sugarloaf Mountain, passing campsites 3 and 4 on the left. Reach the upper end of Sugarloaf Mountain where three more campsites with shelters lie between Sugarloaf and Horseshoe mountains. Campsite 7 offers excellent solitude. These "mountains" are really large hills but can be climbed on erosion-preventing wooden stairs placed on the hillsides.

The second camping area, with sites 8 through 15, is available for equestrian groups and tent campers. It is more open and sandy. Campsites 8 and 9 are in a

> *This unusual eco-system offers free camping and recreation galore.*

RATINGS

Beauty: ✿ ✿ ✿
Privacy: ✿ ✿ ✿ ✿
Spaciousness: ✿ ✿ ✿ ✿ ✿
Quiet: ✿ ✿ ✿
Security: ✿ ✿ ✿
Cleanliness: ✿ ✿ ✿

ADDRESS: Sand Hills State
Forest
P.O. Box 128
Patrick, SC 29584

OPERATED BY: South Carolina
Forestry Commission

INFORMATION: (843) 498-6478;
www.state.sc.us/
forest/refshill.htm

OPEN: Year-round

SITES: 15

EACH SITE HAS: Picnic table, trash
barrel, some also
have covered
shelters

ASSIGNMENT: By reservation and
first come, first
served

REGISTRATION: At forest headquarters

FACILITIES: Vault toilets

PARKING: At campsites only

FEE: None

ELEVATION: 325 feet

RESTRICTIONS: **Pets:** On leash only
Fires: In fire rings
only
Alcohol: Prohibited
Vehicles: None
Other: 14-day stay
limit

loop beside Mountain Pond. The remainder of the sites is in a large loop amid sandy pine woods. Be aware that tent campers are encouraged to use the first seven sites rather than the equestrian area. All the sites here are very large and offer great privacy and more room than anyone would ever need to pitch a tent. The sites with shelters are the most popular. The only other campground amenity is vault toilets, so bring your own water.

The campground traditionally fills only on Easter weekend. Spring and fall are the most popular use periods. Call ahead and you can have your permit mailed to you, or you can pick it up at the forest head-quarters. Or you can try your luck and just stop by the forest headquarters to get a site.

Nearly all campers climb the campground's Horseshoe and Sugarloaf mountains as a matter of course. A 1.7-mile nature trail, pick up the Long Trail trailhead by leaving Mountain Pond and walking toward SC 29, the way you came in. Others will try their luck fishing in Mountain Pond, where bream and bass ply the waters. The state forest has 13 other fish-able ponds. But mountain biking is what's really catch-ing on here.

Sand Hills State Forest has established a mountain biking trail that starts near its headquarters. The trail offers 11 miles of trail biking over four loops, the largest of which is 6 miles. The "Screamer," "Vista," and "Ho Chi Min[h] Trail" are some names that sec-tions of the bike trail have received. A trail permit, which can also be obtained at park headquarters, is required. Bikers and other visitors can also enjoy the adjacent Carolina Hills National Wildlife Refuge, where 100 miles of gravel roads await. These roads are only occasionally used by park personnel and are "edging toward single-track" as the park states. Hiking and driving trails also await. I enjoyed driving around the state forest. (Truth be known I got lost trying a shortcut. Get a map at forest headquarters before you explore.) Nonetheless, I was surprised at the views and the attractive nature of this land. It has so much poten-tial, and with a free campground like Sugarloaf Moun-tain, your base camp is set and waiting for you.

MAP

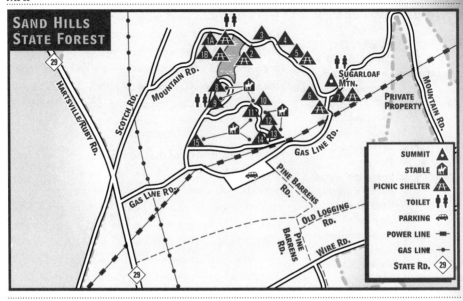

From downtown Cheraw, head south on US 1 for 18 miles to Hartsville/Ruby Road. This road is 0.8 miles past the Sand Hill State Forest Headquarters. Turn right on Hartsville/Ruby Road and follow it for 2.8 miles to Forest Road 63. Turn right on sandy Forest Road 63, Scotch Road, which leaves at an angle, and follow it for 0.5 miles. Veer right on Moutain Road and reach the camping area with sites 1 through 7. The second area (sites 8–15) is off Gas Line Road, leaving SC 29 perpendicular to SC 29, just before Scotch Road.

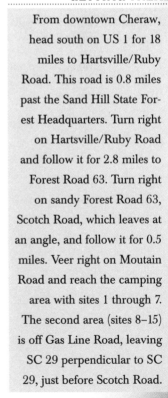

WOODS FERRY
RECREATION AREA

> *This part of the Sumter National Forest is rich in river recreation.*

I N ADDITION TO THE ENTIRE STATE, Woods Ferry Recreation Area is loaded with American history. The adjacent Broad River was once an obstacle to travelers of times past. In 1817, Matthew Woods saw an opportunity, acquiring the land that is now a campground, and constructed a ferry for people, horses, and buggies to cross the truly broad Broad River. During the Civil War, Confederate General Wade Hampton used the ferry while chasing Union General William Sherman during Sherman's infamous March to the Sea that effectively ended the War Between the States. Later, the terrain, like much of the South Carolina Midlands, was logged, and then unsoundly farmed, leading to soil erosion. The U.S. Forest Service took over the depleted lands, managing them for timber and recreation. Bridges replaced the ferry both north and south of the ferry location. Today, Woods Ferry is a rustic recreation area with a quiet campground, hiking, boating, and fishing.

The campground is located along a sloping valley along the Broad River. The valley, moister than the area uplands, flourishes in a forest of oaks, elm, and cedars, with a small understory of trees and bushes. Reaching Camping Loop A first, pass the first two sites as the loop angles up the hillside. The campsites are very large. Reach a high point at campsite 10, which is a double site. The loop then curves past a bathhouse. The widespread campsites don't all have exactly the same amenities, such as lantern posts and such, because the forest service is adding them as funds allow. A factor in picking your site is which particular amenities are available at which sites. The loop flattens out and ends at 18.

Loop B, which is closer to the Broad River than Loop A, has camping units 19 through 30. Head up a hill, crossing wet weather streambeds bordered by

RATINGS

Beauty: ✿ ✿ ✿
Privacy: ✿ ✿ ✿
Spaciousness: ✿ ✿ ✿ ✿
Quiet: ✿ ✿ ✿ ✿
Security: ✿ ✿ ✿
Cleanliness: ✿ ✿ ✿

wood fences to campsite 22 that is a little open. A mini-loop contains the most private sites, including site 29, which is well shaded and close to the day-use area. Each loop has a small bathhouse, with hot showers that is walled on the sides but open to the sky. Water spigots are seemingly everywhere in this campground that rarely—if ever—fills.

Boaters use it occasionally as do hunters, but overall the place is underused. It is a make-your-own-fun campground. My fun started with the day-use area. Located on a flat beside the Broad River, this area has the right combination of sun, shade, grass, and covered picnic shelters (handy in a rain) to enjoy the Broad River. A boat ramp is used by those with johnboats and canoes floating the Broad. You can put in here and travel 6 or 7 miles downstream to the South Sandy boat ramp. A forest service map comes in handy here. Call ahead and order a map before your trip. The nearby Tyger and Enoree rivers are excellent for canoeing, with clear water and narrower, more intimate, streamsheds. The Tyger offers 24 miles of floating while the Enoree offers 36 paddleable miles through the national forest. All three rivers offer freshwater angling.

Also, the Woods Ferry area has a trail system used by hikers, bikers, and horses. It's a little hard to find. Before you take off check out the trail map on the back of the fee station signboard. Three loops can be made of 3.3 miles, 3.7 miles, and 4 miles respectively, offering forest types of the river flood plain and the Piedmont. The first trailhead is about 100 feet behind the fee station signboard as you face it. The second trail access point is harder to find. Look for the painted blazes on the right side of the day-use area road, a little past the covered signboard in the picnic area. The blazes are on two cedar trees side by side. The hand-drawn sketch of the map on the fee station signboard will help. The map may be rudimentary, but it's a lot easier to get around Woods Ferry today than it was over a hundred years ago, when the ferry was in operation.

ADDRESS: Woods Ferry Recreation Area 3557 Whitmire Hwy Union, SC 29379

OPERATED BY: U.S. Forest Service

INFORMATION: (864) 427-9858; www.fs.fed.us/r8/fms

OPEN: Year-round

SITES: 28

EACH SITE HAS: Picnic table, fire ring, some also have barbecue pit, upright grill and/or lantern post

ASSIGNMENT: First come, first served; no reservations

REGISTRATION: Self-registration on-site

FACILITIES: Hot showers, flush toilets, water spigots, vault toilets; showers are shut off November–March

PARKING: At campsites only

FEE: $7 per night

ELEVATION: 400 feet

RESTRICTIONS: Pets: On leash only
Fires: In fire rings only
Alcohol: At campsites only
Vehicles: None
Other: 14-day stay limit

MAP

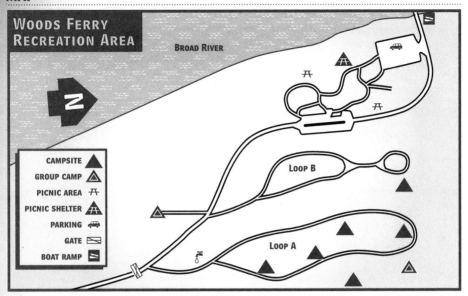

WOODS FERRY RECREATION AREA

BROAD RIVER

N

CAMPSITE
GROUP CAMP
PICNIC AREA
PICNIC SHELTER
PARKING
GATE
BOAT RAMP

LOOP B

LOOP A

GETTING THERE

From Exit 74 on I-26, take SC 34 east for 18 miles to SC 215. Turn left on SC 215 and follow it for 14.5 mile to SC 72. Turn right on SC 72 and follow it for 1.4 miles to SC 25. Turn left on SC 25, Leeds Road, and follow it for 2.1 miles, veer left on SC 49, crossing the railroad tracks, and keep on SC 49 for 3.6 miles to SC 574. Turn left on SC 574 and follow it 3.6 miles to the campground.

SOUTH CAROLINA
LOWCOUNTRY

HONEY HILL CAMPGROUND

THIS CAMPGROUND IS nothing to climb a hill and shout about. However, it is currently the best tent camping area in the Francis Marion National Forest. The forest is named for Revolutionary War Gen. Francis Marion, nicknamed the "Swamp Fox." The forest is an underutilized treasure of South Carolina where adventurers can hike and/or bike the Palmetto Trail at its very beginning, and explores four wilderness swamps in the tidally influenced lowlands just a few miles from the Atlantic Ocean. Consider the campground a way station for exploring as opposed to an end destination in and of itself.

Honey Hill is only 32 feet high, but a little height here in the Lowcountry can mean a lot. The elevation gain from nearby McClellanville to Honey Hill is nearly imperceptible. A fire tower stands next to the campground. Unfortunately it is retired. Pass the tower and enter a gravel loop. Live oaks, hickory, sweetgum, and pines shade the campground. Spanish moss hangs from the trees, and grass grows where the sun breaches the canopy. With sites not being numbered or exactly delineated, the campground is a little disorganized.

All the campsites are on the outside of the loop. The first site is somewhat open and grassy. Circling around past well-separated camps, the final two sites are large and shady and back up to Forest Road 219. The center of the loop has an information kiosk and a pump well. A vault toilet is at the loop's beginning.

The mosquitoes can be troublesome here in Francis Marion National Forest. However the elevation of Honey Hill keeps it drier and less buggy than other campgrounds. Smart forest visitors will call ahead for a bug report and plan their recreation activities during the cooler months. A great time to visit is in fall after the first frost. The forest offers plenty of autumn color to enjoy.

> *Honey Hill is your headquarters for exploring the Lowcountry's Francis Marion National Forest.*

RATINGS

Beauty: ✿ ✿
Privacy: ✿ ✿
Spaciousness: ✿ ✿ ✿ ✿
Quiet: ✿ ✿ ✿
Security: ✿ ✿
Cleanliness: ✿ ✿ ✿

KEY INFORMATION

ADDRESS: Francis Marion
National Forest
P.O. Box 788
McClellanville,
SC 29458

OPERATED BY: U.S. Forest Service

INFORMATION: (843) 887-3257;
www.fs.fed.us/r8/fms

OPEN: Year-round

SITES: 7

EACH SITE HAS: Picnic table, some
also have grills

ASSIGNMENT: First come, first
served; no reserva-
tions

REGISTRATION: None

FACILITIES: Pump well, vault
toilets

PARKING: At campsites only

FEE: None

ELEVATION: 32 feet

RESTRICTIONS: Pets: On leash only
Fires: In fire rings
only
Alcohol: At camp-
sites only
Vehicles: None
Other: 14-day stay
limit

A Francis Marion National Forest map is a must for getting around. Get one before you come or stop at the Sewee Visitor Center on US 17 in Awendaw. The number is (843) 928-3368. The visitor center has its own trails, informative displays, and programs. It pays to call ahead for hiking and paddling information about the forest. Four national forest wilderness areas are just a few miles from Honey Hill. Intrepid adventurers can see all four, but Wambaw Creek Wilderness is the most accessible. Take a 9-mile canoe trip from Still Landing to Echaw Road along a blackwater creek flanked by tupelo and cypress trees. Expect to see wildlife. Consider timing your paddle with the tides.

Little Wambaw Swamp Wilderness, at 5,000 acres, is very primitive. Explorers can follow old built-up tram roads amid swampland. The only catch is the tram bridges have eroded away, making wading a certainty. Wambaw Swamp Wilderness has even less dry ground in its 4,800 acres. According to the forest service this swamp is the least visited locale in the whole state. Hellhole Bay Wilderness has a 5-mile channel that can be canoed during high water. Call ahead about water levels. Nearby Echaw Creek offers more paddling in a non-wilderness setting and is much more user friendly. Start at Pitch Landing and paddle down intimate Echaw Creek to reach the wide Santee River after 3 miles. Then head down Santee River 6 miles to McConnell's Landing.

The Palmetto Trail, South Carolina's master path, begins its journey to the Upcountry here in the Francis Marion. This segment of the Palmetto Trail, formerly known as the Swamp Fox Trail, starts near Buck Hall Campground and heads along Awendaw Creek toward the interior to Halfway Creek and beyond, 27 miles from Buck Hall to the Witherbee Ranger Station. From the ranger station it is 15 more miles to Lake Moultrie. Visit www.palmettoconservation.org for more information on the Palmetto Trail. Then leave the virtual world behind and see the real thing at Honey Hill in the Francis Marion National Forest.

MAP

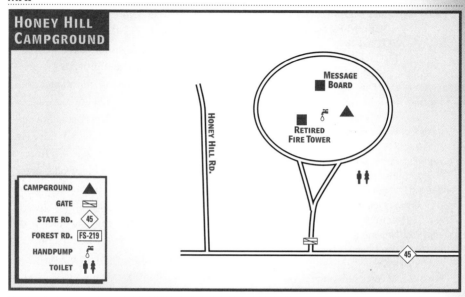

HONEY HILL
CAMPGROUND

MESSAGE
BOARD

RETIRED
FIRE TOWER

HONEY HILL RD.

CAMPGROUND	▲
GATE	⊠
STATE RD.	⟨45⟩
FOREST RD.	FS-219
HANDPUMP	🚰
TOILET	🚹🚺

45

GETTING THERE

From US 17 in McClellanville, take SC 45 for 8.2 miles to the campground, on your left.

HUNTING ISLAND
STATE PARK

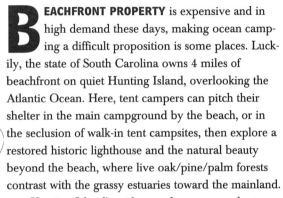

> *This park features South Carolina's longest public beach frontage.*

BEACHFRONT PROPERTY is expensive and in high demand these days, making ocean camping a difficult proposition is some places. Luckily, the state of South Carolina owns 4 miles of beachfront on quiet Hunting Island, overlooking the Atlantic Ocean. Here, tent campers can pitch their shelter in the main campground by the beach, or in the seclusion of walk-in tent campsites, then explore a restored historic lighthouse and the natural beauty beyond the beach, where live oak/pine/palm forests contrast with the grassy estuaries toward the mainland.

Hunting Island's widespread campground set along the Atlantic shoreline attracts tent campers with its natural beauty. The first loop has campsites 1 through 59. Live oaks, palms, and slash pines shade the oceanside sites. This is the land of the RVs, but the tent sites are appealing. If you are going to camp here, go for sites 38 through 55. They are within feet of the beach. The second beachfront loop has campsites 60 through 86. These sites are heavily shaded, too, with more pines than live oaks. The best sites here are 61 through 73, where pine needles, oak leaves, and sand carpet the campsites.

The rear camping area houses campsites 89 through 200, in a series of loops. The woods are thicker here and ancient wooded dunes offer geographic relief to the otherwise flat area. Palmetto and brush add campsite privacy. This rear area also has the two walk-in tent camping areas, where solitude and quiet reign. The first walk-in area, sites T-1 through T-5, leaves the main campground near campsite 162. A sandy path leads to a heavily wooded rolling area, so hilly that tent sites are limited. Some sites have a fire grate in addition to a picnic table. The farthest walk is less than 100 yards but seems a world away from the main campground. The second walk-in tent camping

RATINGS

Beauty: ☆ ☆ ☆ ☆
Privacy: ☆ ☆ ☆
Spaciousness: ☆ ☆ ☆
Quiet: ☆ ☆ ☆ ☆
Security: ☆ ☆ ☆ ☆ ☆
Cleanliness: ☆ ☆ ☆

area, near campsite 177, has sites T-6 through T-10. These are the best tent sites. They are more widespread, larger, and have more level ground among the trees.

A camp store is conveniently located within walking distance of all the sites, and water spigots are located at each walk-in tent area. Eight bath houses are spread throughout the campground. The walk-in sites fill on holiday weekends but are available any weekday. The rest of the campground fills every weekend during summer and occasionally during the week. Only campsites 1 through 40 are reservable. Mosquitoes can be troublesome following rainy periods so call ahead for the latest bug report.

The beach is what drew me to Hunting Island. I enjoyed walking to the north end of the island, then a good way south, stopping to check out the Hunting Island Lighthouse. Built in 1873, the lighthouse and surrounding grounds have been preserved. Enjoy the view from the top of the lighthouse and also the interpretive information about the lighthouse keepers. The lives they led with their families at this solitary outpost assisted ships in avoiding the offshore shoals between Savannah and Charleston. Other park visitors will be surf fishing or angling from the 1,120-foot pier extending into Fripp Island Inlet, in hopes of catching whiting, speckle trout, drum, or flounder.

You can enjoy the beautiful forest via the 8 miles of trails that course through the park's interior. One trail leads from the campground access road to the historic lighthouse area. Another path makes a 6-mile loop to the end of the island by the fishing pier and back. The mainland side of the park features a boardwalk through an estuarine marsh and also has a wildlife viewing area. The most appealing aspect of the park is its pristine natural state and lack of nearby commercialism and high-rise condos. During busy times, the campground itself can seem bustling, but not compared to other beach destinations. Spring and fall are ideal times to enjoy this park, but anytime is better than no time at all.

KEY INFORMATION

ADDRESS: Hunting Island State Park
2555 Sea Island Pkwy
Hunting Island, SC 29920

OPERATED BY: South Carolina State Parks

INFORMATION: (843) 838-2011; www.southcarolina parks.com

OPEN: Tent sites open March–November; campsites 1–86, year-round

SITES: 10 walk-in tent sites, 180 other sites

EACH SITE HAS: Tent sites have picnic table, others have picnic table, water, electricity

ASSIGNMENT: First come, first served and by reservation

REGISTRATION: At park store

FACILITIES: Hot showers, flush toilet, water spigots

PARKING: At campsites and at walk-in tent camping parking areas

FEE: $11.50 walk-in tent sites; others, $23 per night March–October, $19 per night November–February

ELEVATION: Sea level

RESTRICTIONS: Pets: On leash only
Fires: In fire rings only
Alcohol: Prohibited
Vehicles: Two cars per walk-in tent site
Other: 14-day stay limit

MAP

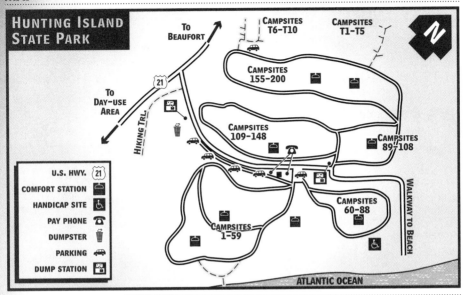

HUNTING ISLAND STATE PARK

To BEAUFORT

CAMPSITES T6-T10

CAMPSITES T1-T5

CAMPSITES 155-200

To DAY-USE AREA

HIKING TRL.

CAMPSITES 109-148

CAMPSITES 89-108

CAMPSITES 60-88

CAMPSITES 1-59

WALKWAY TO BEACH

ATLANTIC OCEAN

U.S. HWY. 21
COMFORT STATION
HANDICAP SITE
PAY PHONE
DUMPSTER
PARKING
DUMP STATION

GETTING THERE

From Exit 33 on I-95, take US 21 south for 42 miles, through the town of Beaufort and staying with US 21 to Hunting Island. Turn left on Campground Road to reach the campground.

HUNTINGTON BEACH
STATE PARK

CAMPERS COME TO **H**UNTINGTON **B**EACH for a variety of reasons. Many like to enjoy the beach and other natural aspects of this 2,500 acres preserve in a fast developing coast. Others like to relax in the campground after seeking activities outside the park. Either way they enjoy this getaway, one of the limited public beach camping locales in the state of South Carolina. This one has the added benefit, or detraction, of being 16 miles from the heart of Myrtle Beach.

The campground, a short walk from the beach, has two large loops with a separate walk-in tent camping area. The first loop has the sites closest to the beach in a mix of sun and shade from planted cedars and live oaks. This is the land of the RV, but has some good sites. Make reservations for odd-numbered campsites 1 through 31 in this loop. A recreation building is located near campsite 19, and is convenient for those inevitable summer thunderstorms. Avoid sites 74 through 88, and 90 through 102, which are located on crossroads within the loop. Most sites on the remainder of the first loop have at least one shade tree. Woe to those stuck in a sunny site on a hot South Carolina summer day. The second loop has sites farthest from the ocean. Many of them have thick brush between sites, offering good campsite privacy, but little overhead shade.

Try to get one of the walk-in tent sites if you can; they are first come, first served. To reach them, leave the walk-in parking area and follow a sandy trail past a water spigot to the sites. Campsite T-1 lies beneath a large live oak. T-2 is more open. T-3 has shade from pines and live oaks. T-4 is a little on the small side. T-5 has good shade and is large. T-6 is the farthest back and set amid privacy-giving brush.

This popular state park stays busy throughout the warmer part of the year. That means it fills weekends

> *This oceanside park is close—but not too close—to Myrtle Beach.*

RATINGS

Beauty: ✪ ✪ ✪
Privacy: ✪ ✪ ✪
Spaciousness: ✪ ✪ ✪
Quiet: ✪ ✪ ✪ ✪
Security: ✪ ✪ ✪ ✪ ✪
Cleanliness: ✪ ✪ ✪

ADDRESS:	Huntington Beach State Park 16148 Ocean Hwy Murrells Inlet, SC 29576
OPERATED BY:	South Carolina State Parks
INFORMATION:	(843) 237-4440; www.southcarolina parks.com
OPEN:	Year-round
SITES:	6 walk-in tent sites, 133 other sites
EACH SITE HAS:	Walk-in sites have picnic table, fire ring; 123 have water and electricity, 10 also have sewer
ASSIGNMENT:	First come, first served and by reservation
REGISTRATION:	At office/gift shop
FACILITIES:	Hot showers, flush toilets, water spigots
PARKING:	At campsites and at walk-in tent camping parking area
FEE:	April–October, tent sites $11 per night, others $23 and $25; November–March, tent sites $9.50, others $20 and $22
ELEVATION:	Sea level
RESTRICTIONS:	Pets: On leash only Fires: In fire rings only Alcohol: Prohibited Vehicles: None Other: 14-day stay limit

from March to September, and many weekdays during the peak of summer. Many sites can be reserved, especially those closest to the beach. These beachside sites are often filled with RVs—location has its price, but proximity to an ocean breeze will cut down on insects when they are bothersome, usually following rainy periods. The walk-in tent sites offer much more privacy and the experience tent campers are after. A camp store is conveniently located inside the park.

Huntington Beach State Park prides itself on its naturalist programs. Checking out the alligators on the park causeway is a popular pastime. Let park personnel inform you about these ancient creatures. Other programs cover birding, the salt marsh, seashells, whales, dolphins, and the historic homesite known as Atalaya. This winter home of park benefactors Collis and Anna Huntington is modeled after houses on the Spanish Mediterranean coast. Rangers lead tours of this home and three different park programs are held during the busy season, March through September. The park education center offers more learning experiences.

Three miles of beachfront attract ocean enthusiasts who shell, surf fish or just relax while listening to the waves roll in. A jetty at the north end of Huntington Beach is also a popular fishing spot. Some will be hiking the two nature trails or kayaking the saltwater marsh. But many others will be enjoying the attractions of the nearby tourist destinations at Myrtle Beach, ranging from putt-putt golf to dinner shows to water slides. Shoppers will be looking for the perfect grass basket from the area or a hammock from Pawleys Island. So, whether you prefer to shop and act the part of the hokey tourist or you just like to enjoy the undeveloped shoreline, Huntington Beach may be the place for you.

MAP

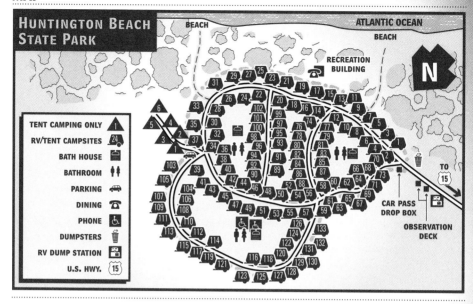

HUNTINGTON BEACH STATE PARK

BEACH

ATLANTIC OCEAN

BEACH

RECREATION BUILDING

N

TENT CAMPING ONLY	▲ 1
RV/TENT CAMPSITES	24
BATH HOUSE	
BATHROOM	��
PARKING	🚐
DINING	☎
PHONE	♿
DUMPSTERS	
RV DUMP STATION	
U.S. HWY.	15

CAR PASS DROP BOX

OBSERVATION DECK

TO 15

GETTING THERE

From Myrtle Beach, take US 17 south for 16 miles to the state park, on your left.

LITTLE PEE DEE
STATE PARK

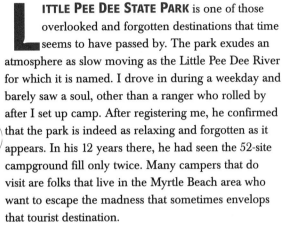

> *Time slows down at this backwater park.*

LITTLE PEE DEE STATE PARK is one of those overlooked and forgotten destinations that time seems to have passed by. The park exudes an atmosphere as slow moving as the Little Pee Dee River for which it is named. I drove in during a weekday and barely saw a soul, other than a ranger who rolled by after I set up camp. After registering me, he confirmed that the park is indeed as relaxing and forgotten as it appears. In his 12 years there, he had seen the 52-site campground fill only twice. Many campers that do visit are folks that live in the Myrtle Beach area who want to escape the madness that sometimes envelops that tourist destination.

The campground is laid out in a grand loop along the shores of Lake Norton. The sandy road leads to sand parking spurs. Many pines and oaks grow overhead while dogwoods are a prevalent understory tree. Oddly, the first two campsites in the loop are 49 and 50. Then the numbering becomes more conventional. Two small sub-loops spur from the main loop. Curve toward the lake, passing a picnic area with a covered shelter near campsite 7 and pass some lakeside sites. Campsites here have a raked sand floor with needles and oak leaves marking their perimeter. The sites are very large and well separated from one another. Since the campground rarely gets crowded, privacy isn't much of an issue, meaning you likely won't have a neighbor at the campsite next door.

The sub-loop curves away from the lake and joins the main loop and lakeside sites resume with site 20. The next few campsites, which offer great vistas of Lake Norton, are the campground's most coveted. Leaving the lake again, the official tent sites start with campsite 33. These are the nonelectric sites and are cheaper and in less demand than the electric sites.

RATINGS

Beauty: ✿ ✿ ✿
Privacy: ✿ ✿ ✿
Spaciousness: ✿ ✿ ✿ ✿
Quiet: ✿ ✿ ✿ ✿
Security: ✿ ✿ ✿ ✿ ✿
Cleanliness: ✿ ✿ ✿ ✿

I stayed in campsite 34, and was the only tent camper that night, enjoying a piney fire that warmed me. A front moved in later, warming the air and bringing rain. Breaking camp in the rain is never fun, but is an element of tent camping if you do it often enough.

The Beaver Pond Nature Trail begins just past campsite 40. It is more of a leg-stretching path than a bona fide hiking trail, though it does loop to a beaver pond. The tent sites here have thicker woods around them, are less used, and they angle ever so slightly downhill toward Lake Norton. Complete the loop near some very large tent sites suitable for a family gathering. Two bath houses center the loop. The newer one is heated, a fact I appreciated during my late fall trip. A play area is also in the loop center.

This part of South Carolina, Dillon County, is rural and relaxing. Little Pee Dee's 835 acres, stretched along the Little Pee Dee River, mark the apex of this quietness. A park lake, adding more aquatic beauty, complements the river and adjoining swamp. The damming of Bell Swamp Branch and Indian Pot Branch forms Lake Norton. The 54-acre impoundment is a "no gas motors" lake, keeping the atmosphere serene. It does have a boat launch, however, and offers boat rentals for those who want to tour the lake or do some freshwater fishing. Anglers can also fish from the banks of the lake or from the near the lake dam.

The park's namesake, the Little Pee Dee River, is also a boating possibility. The Little Pee Dee is a fine example of a coastal plain blackwater river. Cypress trees and tupelo line much of the river, as do sandbars, which are great for picnicking or relaxing. The river is tough to access from the park bridge but boasts landings and accesses nearby. Instead of trying to figure out all the particulars of a canoe trip why not leave it to the outfitters? Betwixt the Rivers, based in nearby Marion, South Carolina, offers trips of varying lengths. They can be reached at (843) 423-1919. Make sure and have a little extra time on your hands, as life is slow and relaxing in this part of the Palmetto State.

ADDRESS:	Little Pee Dee State Park 1298 State Park Road Dillon, SC 29536
OPERATED BY:	South Carolina State Parks
INFORMATION:	(843) 774-8872; www.southcarolina parks.com
OPEN:	Year-round
SITES:	18 tent sites, 32 other sites
EACH SITE HAS:	Tent sites have picnic table, fire ring, water
ASSIGNMENT:	First come, first served; no reservations
REGISTRATION:	Ranger will come by and register you
FACILITIES:	Hot showers, flush toilets
PARKING:	At campsites only
FEE:	Tent sites, $7 per night, $12 others
ELEVATION:	100 feet
RESTRICTIONS:	**Pets:** On leash only **Fires:** In fire rings only **Alcohol:** Prohibited **Vehicles:** None **Other:** 14-day stay limit

MAP

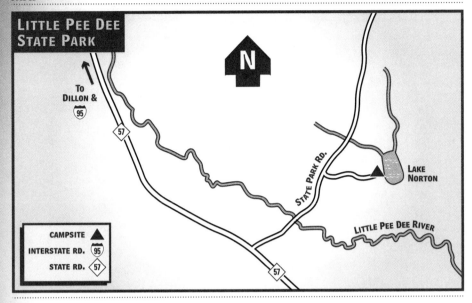

LITTLE PEE DEE STATE PARK

To DILLON & 95

57

STATE PARK RD.

LAKE NORTON

LITTLE PEE DEE RIVER

57

CAMPSITE
INTERSTATE RD. 95
STATE RD. 57

GETTING THERE

From Exit 193 on I-95 near Dillon, take SC 57 south as it twists and turns through the town of Dillon and stay with SC 57 for a total of 11.2 miles from the interstate, to reach State Park Road. Turn left on State Park Road and follow it 2 miles to the state park entrance, on your right.

APPENDICES

APPENDIX A
CAMPING EQUIPMENT
CHECKLIST

Except for the large and bulky items on this list, I keep a plastic storage container full of the essentials for car camping so they're ready to go when I am. I make a last-minute check of the inventory, resupply anything that's low or missing, and away I go.

COOKING UTENSILS
Bottle opener
Bottles of salt, pepper, spices, sugar,
    cooking oil and maple syrup in water-
    proof, spillproof containers
Can opener
Cups, plastic or tin
Corkscrew
Cups, plastic or tin
Dish soap (biodegradable), sponge, towel
Flatware
Food of your choice
Frying pan, spatula
Fuel for stove
Lighter, matches in waterproof container
Plates
Pocketknife
Fire starter
Pot with lid
Stove
Tin foil
Wooden spoon

FIRST AID KIT
Band-Aids
Antibiotic cream
Gauze pads
Aspirin or ibuprofen
Insect repellent
Moleskin
Sunscreen/lip balm
Diphenhydramine (Benadryl)

Tweezers
Tape, waterproof adhesive

SLEEPING GEAR
Pillow
Sleeping bag
Sleeping pad, inflatable or insulated
Tent with ground tarp and rainfly

MISCELLANEOUS
Bath soap (biodegradable), washcloth
    and towel
Camp chair
Candles
Cooler
Deck of cards
Flashlight/headlamp
Lantern
Maps (road, trail, topographic, etc.)
Paper towels
Plastic zip-top bags
Sunglasses
Toilet paper
Water bottle
Wool blanket

OPTIONAL
Barbecue grill
Binoculars
Field guides on bird, plant, and
    wildlife identification
Fishing rod and tackle
GPS

APPENDIX B
SOURCES OF
INFORMATION

South Carolina

FRANCIS MARION AND SUMTER NATIONAL FOREST
4931 Broad River Road
Columbia, SC 29212
(828) 257-4200
www.fs.fed.us/r8/fms

KINGS MOUNTAIN NATIONAL MILITARY PARK
2625 Park Road
Blacksburg, SC 29702
(864) 936-7921
www.nps.gov/kimo

SOUTH CAROLINA DEPARTMENT OF TOURISM
1205 Pendleton Street
Columbia, SC 29201
(803) 734-1062
www.discoversouthcarolina.com

SOUTH CAROLINA STATE PARKS
1205 Pendleton Street
Columbia, SC 29201
(888) 88-PARKS
www.southcarolinaparks.com

U.S. ARMY CORPS OF ENGINEERS
U.S. Army Corps of Engineers
Savannah District
P.O. Box 889
Savannah, GA 40201
(912) 652-5822
www.sas.usace.army.mil

North Carolina

GREAT SMOKY MOUNTAINS NATIONAL PARK
107 Park Headquarters Road
Gatlinburg, TN 37320
(865) 436-1200
www.nps.gov/grsm

NATIONAL FORESTS IN NORTH CAROLINA
160A Zillicoa Street
P.O. Box 2750
Asheville, NC 28802
(828) 257-4200
www.cs.unca.edu/nfsnc

BLUE RIDGE PARKWAY
199 Hemphill Knob Road
Asheville, NC 28803
(828) 271-4779
www.nps.gov/blri

NORTH CAROLINA DEPARTMENT OF TOURISM
301 North Wilmington Street
Raleigh, NC 27601
(800) VISIT-NC
www.visitnc.com

NORTH CAROLINA STATE PARKS
1615 MSC
Raleigh, NC 27699
(919) 733-PARK
www.ncparks.net

ABOUT THE
AUTHOR

Johnny Molloy is an outdoor writer based in Tennessee. A native Tennessean, he was born in Memphis and moved to Knoxville in 1980 to attend the University of Tennessee. It was in the Great Smoky Mountains National Park where he developed his love of the natural world that has become the primary focus of his life. Molloy has averaged over 100 nights in the wild per year since the early 1980s, backpacking, canoeing and camping throughout our country. He has spent over 650 nights in the Smokies alone, where he cultivated his woodsmanship and expertise on those lofty mountains.

Now, Molloy employs his love of the outdoors as an occupation. The results of his efforts are both guidebooks and true adventure story books covering the United States from Florida to Wisconsin to Colorado and many points in between. Molloy has also written numerous articles for magazines and websites. He continues to write to this day and travel extensively to all four corners of the United States, endeavoring in a variety of outdoor pursuits. For the latest on Molloy, visit www.johnnymolloy.com.